LEARNING THROUGH PLAY

Water

AVRIL HARPLEY
& ANN ROBERTS

Published by Scholastic Ltd,
Villiers House,
Clarendon Avenue,
Leamington Spa,
Warwickshire CV32 5PR
Text © Avril Harpley and Ann Roberts
© 1996 Scholastic Ltd
6 7 8 9 0   0 1 2 3 4 5

Authors
Avril Harpley and Ann Roberts

Editor
Jane Bishop

Assistant Editor
Sally Gray

Series designer
Lynne Joesbury

Designer
Lynda Murray

Illustrations
Lorna Kent

Cover photograph
Fiona Pragoff

Designed using Aldus Pagemaker

British Library Cataloguing-in-Publication Data
A catalogue record for this book is available from the British Library.

ISBN 0-590-53637-0

CONTENTS

INTRODUCTION 5

CHAPTER 1: COMMUNICATION, LANGUAGE AND LITERACY

FLOATING LETTERS 11
THREE BILLY GOATS 12
INCY WINCY SPIDER 13
WHAT'S THAT NOISE? 14
UNDERWATER CAVE 15
OUT AND ABOUT 16
THE LAUNDRETTE 17
THE HAIRDRESSER'S 18

CHAPTER 2: MATHEMATICAL DEVELOPMENT

TEN GREEN BOTTLES 19
STEPPING STONES 20
SHAPE IT 21
DUCKS 22
TEA PARTY 23
FIVE SPECKLED FROGS 24
SEAWORLD 25
MARVELLOUS MIXTURES 26

CHAPTER 3: PERSONAL, SOCIAL AND EMOTIONAL DEVELOPMENT

BATHTIME 27
DOLPHIN 28
SOS 29
SEA HARVEST 30
GOLDFISH 31
PIRATE'S PANIC 32
GALA TIME 33
GAME TIME 34

CHAPTER 4: KNOWLEDGE AND UNDERSTANDING OF THE WORLD

RAINBOW COLOURS 35
CROW'S PROBLEM 36
UP AND DOWN 37
MOP IT UP 38
SPRAYS 39
BUBBLES 40
THE BOAT RACE 41
CROCODILE WORLD 42

CHAPTER 5: PHYSICAL DEVELOPMENT

WATER WHEEL   43
CATCH THE SPIDER   44
APPLE BOBBING   45
MILKSHAKES   46
FILL IT UP   47
PHANTOM PAINTER   48
PADDLING POOL   49
WASHDAY BLUES   50

CHAPTER 6: CREATIVE DEVELOPMENT

MARBLE GOO   51
THE BOTTLE SHOP   52
ITALIA   53
JELLY WOBBLE   54
WHISK   55
IT'S A COLOURFUL WORLD   56
ICELAND   57
I'M A LITTLE TEAPOT   58

PHOTOCOPIABLES

THE HAIRDRESSER'S   59
TEN GREEN BOTTLES   60
SEA HARVEST   61
PIRATE'S PANIC   62
CROW'S PROBLEM   63
MILKSHAKES   64

INTRODUCTION

All children love to play with water. They are fascinated and attracted by water. They need opportunities to expand their interest by playing in and near water. Some young children may never have had opportunities to explore first hand the water outside the home, some have never been to the seaside. Their knowledge will be limited to washing routines and the rain.

Water provides a rich source of unique properties to explore, investigate and discover. It is through the senses that children learn and water can offer a total sensory experience; it runs through their fingers, they can immerse their whole bodies in it. Water can change shape and texture, it can take on different colours and smells.

Learning through play

Children learn by imitating activities they see at home; bathing babies, washing clothes, watering the garden and whilst they become involved in this imitative play they learn how things behave and how the world works.

Very early play with water will take place at bathtime, with children splashing and sploshing in the secure and caring environment. A different kind of learning will take place outdoors as they enjoy boisterous play, taking risks by dodging a squirting hosepipe. Time spent repeatedly filling and emptying containers will not be wasted as children learn about quantity and capacity. At the same time they will be developing co-ordination skills, gripping and grasping when they carefully pour the liquid from one container to another.

How to use this book

The ideas and activities in this book will provide many weeks of constructive play that will stretch children intellectually, physically and creatively. Each chapter has a specific focus and each covers one of the areas suggested for under-fives by the Qualifications and Curriculum Authority (QCA) in its publication *Curriculum guidance for the foundation stage*. The six chapters are Communication, language and literacy, Mathematical development, Personal, social and emotional development, Knowledge and understanding of the world, Physical development and Creative development.

For example Chapter One covers Communication, language and literacy, so whilst the children play in the water, ideas are provided to advance their language skills. At the same time the children will be

acquiring additional skills, such as knowledge about water, co-operative play with other children and possibly some mathematical concepts.

There is one activity per page and each has an identified learning objective. Each activity also details group size, what you need and setting up as well as what to do. The activities are pitched at a 'typical' four year old. Ideas are provided for younger, less mature children and also to extend older children. On page ten there is a photocopiable web showing all the activities in the book and their page references. The book finishes with six photocopiable sheets to link with the activities.

Planning and preparation

Careful planning is essential, not only to get value out of the activity but also because water play can get messy. You may wish to plan several weeks in advance, arranging to provide a range of different experiences. For example during week one you may use plain water, in week two add foam (CARE! Some children have allergies to foam or bubbles), in week three you could introduce floating and sinking.

You can change the colour of water by adding vegetable dyes. (CARE! When using vegetable dyes the adult should test before use. Check for density and permanence. Some dyes may colour children's hands.) You could also make the water fizz with baking soda, add bubbles or ice-cubes. The same activities can then be explored in new ways to extend children's experiences or confirm their emerging ideas and concepts.

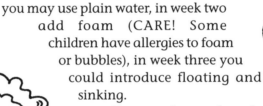

How you organise the size of the group can influence the success of the activities. Ideally each child should feel comfortable standing around the tray and be able to reach and participate. Most of the activities in this book will benefit from a small group situation of four to six children, which will allow all the children to take part and contribute to discussions. Depending on their stage of development and their personalities some children may prefer to work alone, others like to play alongside or just stand and watch, which can also be valuable. Often a pair will work well helping each other and spurring on ideas. Group work can also be valuable as the children will share ideas. Some children will take the initiative moving the whole group's thinking forward.

Talking is an essential part of all the activities. Look for and encourage times when the children are working collaboratively, taking turns and sharing with each other. You will find that water play provides opportunities to observe how children are thinking, how eager they are to experiment as well as developing their language and vocabulary skills.

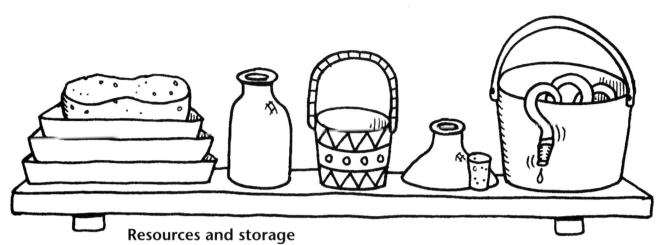

Resources and storage

You will need a large container for the water. Commercially produced water trays range from simple structures to elaborate arrangements with canals, bridges and water wheels. A plug hole in the tray is useful, and a shelf to keep equipment on is also a good idea.

Start collecting a variety of plastic food containers in all shapes and sizes, with wide and narrow necks. Pierce holes in some to make interesting sprays and jets. Make a funnel by cutting the top off a plastic detergent bottle. Cut 10cms beyond the shoulder of the bottle.

Gather together jugs, large and small bowls, buckets, balloon whisks, watering cans, sprinklers and sprays. Build up a store of sponges, pipes, tubing and corks, as well as small water play toys: mermaids, pirates and treasure. Ferns, rocks, shells and pebbles are also useful. Make sure you have some objects that will float and others that definitely sink!

Store all the resources so that they are easily accessible, labelled clearly and ready to use. Wheeled vegetable racks are useful for storage as they can be brought out when required and then tucked away. It is easy to see what is in the baskets and they are at a suitable height for young children.

Do not put everything out at once, young children find it difficult with too many choices. Select the items most suitable to enrich the particular activity and keep some others as surprises.

Keep all the resources clean and in good condition, not only for health purposes but also so they are inviting and attractive to the children. The water will need to be changed frequently to keep it clean and fresh.

As part of the learning process children should be encouraged to clean, tidy up and return resources. Keep a mop and bucket, layers of newspaper and a sponge close by to mop up spills quickly. Have a squeegee mop available for the children to use. Take care with plastic sheeting as it becomes slippery when wet.

Make sure the children wear aprons and roll up their sleeves. Some children are very anxious about not getting their clothes wet or dirty. Ensure these children have an apron and try to arrange to have an adult close by them for additional security.

In spite of all your precautions children will sometimes get wet, so have a spare set of clothes available. Whenever possible engage in water activities outdoors.

The adult's role

Some days the children will be happy just to handle the water, getting to know how it behaves, watching how water moves, using their senses. Other days they will need more support from an adult. Questioning is a vital technique. You need to be non judgmental and accept the children's answers even if they are incorrect. Further questions from you can help to clarify their thoughts. Use encouragement to help them think aloud, to explain and interpret ideas. Ask: What would happen if...? What difference do you think it will make if you...? Can you think of other ways to...?

Make some of your questions unusual, ask: Could you carry the water in your pocket? How can you share out the water? Could you cut it with the scissors? Some children need to be encouraged to join in and can benefit from the security of having an adult close by. Join in and talk through the activity, giving a commentary as you play alongside. Once they are settled you can fade away and allow them to experiment. Give them time to try to work out solutions. By listening and observing, you will learn a lot about what they know, how they tackle problems, where they need to go next.

Your presence and interest gives the activity value in the eyes of a child. When an adult is there the activity is seen as important. Give genuine praise when appropriate. Intervene if you observe a problem that cannot be reconciled or solved, for example if children are disrupting or disturbing others or if there is a safety risk.

Observation and assessment

When children are motivated by an activity and clearly involved, it provides an ideal opportunity for you to stand back and observe them. You will hear and see children using language and experiences that they have assimilated. You will find out how they are able to work together, which children take the initiative and which are feeling hesitant. Many of your observations will happen unexpectedly and it is useful to carry a small notebook to jot down events.

Assessment needs to be carefully planned and to have a focus. You need to find out what the children are learning, what they have learned so far, what they can do well, what they should do next. This will also help you know if your resources and equipment are appropriate, if the activity is stimulating and interesting to the children and what elements you need to change.

To assess progress you could use the learning objective described for each activity as your focus. For example, if assessing the children in the activity 'Crocodile world' on page 42, you could record their understanding of floating and sinking objects. Before you begin, prepare a simple grid with the children's names down one side. At the top of the page write the activity, the learning objective, the time and date. You can decide whether to observe the group as a whole or concentrate on one or two children. Observe for two to five minutes and concentrate on what is actually happening and what language is being used. Make notes on the grid to remind you of the progress of each child in the group. Your observations may cause you to intervene immediately with questions to lead the children's play or to present them with a challenge. It might be that the observation throws up the need for extra equipment or to add something new to stimulate play in the activity.

Make notes of the need for further practice or reinforcing experiences to help the children progress. Share your observations with your colleagues.

Health and safety

Throughout the book you will find a CARE! warning where special caution should be taken. Before you start any water play, teach the children some basic rules.

These could include:
● do not drink the water;
● do not throw the water around;
● clean up spills as soon as they happen.

In addition, bear in mind:
● when using empty plastic containers, wash and rinse them well to remove any harmful substances;
● avoid using glass bottles unless under close supervision;
● some children's skin may react to detergents;
● measure out detergents as required and keep these in containers with secure lids;
● if the children spend a long time with hands in the water tray provide a towel and a neutral hand cream;
● make sure any staff avoid lifting heavy equipment on their own.

Links with home

Involve parents whenever possible with the work you are doing. If parents are aware that the children are learning through water play they can support the activities at home.

Inform parents about what you intend to cover over the coming weeks and what the learning objectives are. At home parents can build on these at bath time, when washing clothes or dishes or visits out and about. Parents may also be able to help with collecting resources and they may be willing to provide suitable clothing.

By co-operation and communication between parents and your group, children should have a wide and interesting variety of water activities to explore and enjoy.

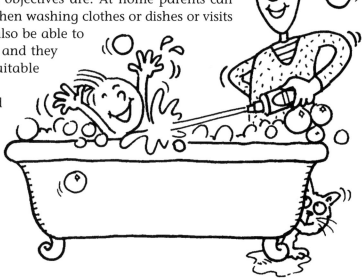

COMMUNICATION, LANGUAGE AND LITERACY
Floating letters, page 11
Three Billy goats, page 12
Incy wincy spider, page 13
What's that noise?, page 14
Underwater cave, page 15
Out and about, page 16
The laundrette, page 17
The hairdresser's, page 18

PERSONAL, SOCIAL AND EMOTIONAL DEVELOPMENT
Bathtime, page 27
Dolphin, page 28
SOS, page 29
Sea harvest, page 30
Goldfish, page 31
Pirate's panic, page 32
Gala time, page 33
Game time, page 34

MATHEMATICAL DEVELOPMENT
Ten green bottles, page 19
Stepping stones, page 20
Shape it, page 21
Ducks, page 22
Tea party, page 23
Five speckled frogs, page 24
Seaworld, page 25
Marvellous mixtures, page 26

WATER

PHYSICAL DEVELOPMENT
Water wheel, page 43
Catch the spider, page 44
Apple bobbing, page 45
Milkshakes, page 46
Fill it up, page 47
Phantom painter, page 48
Paddling pool, page 49
Washday blues, page 50

KNOWLEDGE AND UNDERSTANDING OF THE WORLD
Rainbow colours, page 35
Crow's problem, page 36
Up and down, page 37
Mop it up, page 38
Sprays, page 39
Bubbles, page 40
The boat race, page 41
Crocodile world, page 42

CREATIVE DEVELOPMENT
Marble goo, page 51
The bottle shop, page 52
Italia, page 53
Jelly wobble, page 54
Whisk, page 55
It's a colourful world, page 56
Iceland, page 57
I'm a little teapot, page 58

Children's language and literacy skills using water play as a stimulus are developed here. Many familiar rhymes and stories are used to encourage speaking, listening and oral storytelling skills. Activities such as 'Floating letters' help children to begin to recognise the sounds and letters of the alphabet.

FLOATING LETTERS

Learning objective
To recognise letters of the alphabet and to practise the sounds which correspond with them.

Group size
Four to six children.

What you need
Water container, packs of foam letters, a selection of alphabet books.

Setting up
Half fill the water container. Put one set of letters into the water and keep another set aside.

What to do
Start by allowing the children some time to play with the letters in the water tray on their own. Let them collect up and identify them for themselves. Hold up one letter from your set and ask the children to find the one which matches from the water set. Next, find two quite different letters such as an 'o' and an 'h' and ask the children if these are the same, or different. Select one of the letters and ask the children to copy the shape using a finger in the air or in the water. Repeat this with two more letters. Now try two shapes which are similar, a 'd' and a 'p' for example. Encourage the children to tell you how the shapes are different and ask them to try and make the shapes in the water.

Questions to ask
Is your letter the same as mine? Do you know what this letter is called? What sound does it make? Can you think of a word/name which starts with this letter?

For younger children
These children may find it difficult to separate the phonic sound of a letter and the name of the letter. Help them to concentrate on their own initial letter and the name of it and give them plenty of practise with this first. Draw the shape of the letter on the child's hand and help them to make the same shape in the water tray.

For older children
Encourage them to find the initial letter for their first name in the water tray. If they are able, let them pick out letters to make words from the water tray.

Follow-up activities
● Print with the foam letters using paint or draw around their outlines.
● Make a collection of pictures and match initial letters to them.
● Play sound lotto.

THREE BILLY GOATS

Learning objective
To listen to a familiar story and to re-tell it using props.

Group size
Whole group for the story; four children at the water tray at a time.

What you need
The story of *Three Billy Goats Gruff* (Ladybird), a water container, rocks, pieces of wood for a bridge, three toy goats of different sizes and a troll (this could be made out of Plasticine).

Setting up
Cover the bottom of the tray with water. Place the rocks and stones at either side to make a base for the pieces of wood which will form the bridge. Hide the troll under the bridge.

What to do
Tell the story to the whole group, and encourage them to join in with the repetitions throughout. Use different voices to represent each goat and for the troll. Once the children are familiar with the story take them in groups of four to the water tray. Ask the group of children to tell you the story and to each move a toy goat across the bridge in the water tray as they tell it (the fourth child can 'operate' the troll!). Prompt them or remind them of the story if they can't remember certain parts.

Use the opportunity to develop the children's vocabulary. Ask the children to put the three goats in order of size and encourage them to use comparative vocabulary, such as 'this one is smaller'. Check and develop their understanding of prepositional vocabulary by asking them to put the goats: on the bridge, under the bridge and in the water!

Questions to ask
Why did the goats want to cross the bridge? Could they have crossed the water in any other way? How did the goats trick the troll? What would happen if a goat fell in the water? Do you think goats are able to swim?

For younger children
Take part in the re-telling of the story with younger children, by 'operating' one of the goats and helping them to remember the order of events.

For older children
Use different voices to say phrases from the story and see if the children can identify the character. Let them use information books about farm animals to find out why farmers keep goats.

Follow-up activities
● Paint scenes from the story and display them in their correct sequence on the wall.
● Make model trolls and goats from play dough or clay.
● Gather all the toy farm animals available and ask the children to group them by type, or to sort them in order of size.

INCY WINCY SPIDER

Learning objective
To listen and respond to a familiar rhyme.

Group size
Up to four children.

What you need
Water container, a plastic pipe or tube, a watering can or plastic jug, assortment of plastic spiders, Plasticine, a copy of the poem 'Incy Wincy Spider'.

Setting up
Half fill the water tray. Fix the tube/pipe so that the children can reach it and secure it firmly to the side of the tray using Plasticine. Fill the watering can/jug but make sure the children can lift it.

What to do
Read the poem through to the whole group a few times, modelling the actions. Emphasise the words 'up', 'down' and 'out'. As they become familiar with the poem let them join in with the key words.

In small groups, pairs or individually, let the children work at the water tray playing with the spiders. Show them how to wash the spiders down through the pipe using the watering can. Let them experiment with different sized spiders to see which work best. Encourage them to continue saying the poem aloud as they play with the spiders and water.

Questions to ask
Why did the spider fall down? How much water do you need to pour to wash the spiders out?

For younger children
Young children will enjoy playing with the water and letting it trickle over their hands. Reinforce the words 'up' and 'down' in other situations, such as, when the children are playing on the slide, see-saw or climbing frame.

For older children
Talk about how Incy and Wincy rhyme and see if the children can think of other nursery rhymes which do the same, for example 'Georgie Porgie', 'Humpty Dumpty' and 'Hickory Dickory'.

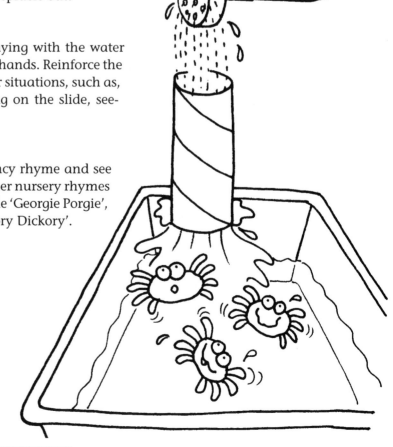

Follow-up activities
● Make an obstacle course for the children to climb up, over and down.
● Say 'Little Miss Muffet' together and discuss why she was frightened by the spider.
● Make pop-up spiders using the toy spiders attached to a lollipop stick, inside a yoghurt pot.

WHAT'S THAT NOISE?

Learning objective
To encourage listening skills and to develop vocabulary to describe experiences.

Group size
Individuals, pairs and small groups.

What you need
Water tray, assortment of water containers in different sizes.

Setting up
Half fill the tray with water. Provide the containers.

What to do
Make sure the children are silent and listening carefully. Select one of the containers and pour water from it into the tray. Listen together to the sound it makes. Next choose a different container and go through the same process. Ask the children which one makes the loudest sound, the first container or the second. Let them experiment themselves with the collection of containers, listening carefully for the variation in sound produced. If they try and use too many of the containers at once, intervene as they will be unable to differentiate between the sounds if too much is going on. After a while change the depth of the water in the tray and see if they think this makes a difference to the sounds they are producing.

   Listen to their explanations of the sounds they produce. See what words they use to describe the sounds (louder, quieter), perhaps they will find their own descriptive words (splashier, sploshier). Encourage them to tell you about the differences they have found, extending their vocabulary and ideas.

Questions to ask
Which containers made loud noises? Which made quieter noises? Do you know why? What was different about the containers? How can you make soft sounds in the water? Does it make any difference if the water in the tray is deep or shallow?

For younger children
Let them try swishing the water with brushes or a whisk, and use tubes to blow bubbles in the water to make a variety of sounds. Ask the younger children to differentiate between loud and soft sounds only. Encourage them to listen carefully.

For older children
See if they can control the flow of water to make dripping sounds. Provide different surfaces for the children to drop water on to, such as a tin lid or a piece of fabric. Encourage descriptive vocabulary to explain the exact sound made, rather then just 'loud' or 'soft'.

Follow-up activities
● Make an audio tape of different commonly heard sounds such as the rain falling, water gushing from a tap.
● Discuss important sounds such as bells, alarms, fire-engines and ambulance sirens.
● Improvise percussion instruments using spoons and beaters.

UNDERWATER CAVE

What you need
The Little Mermaid, Hans Christian Andersen (Penguin), a water container, stones, gravel, rocks, shells, a toy mermaid and other play people and objects including pirates/ fishes/ boats, sequins, colourful buttons, treasure box.

Setting up
Place the rocks and stones in the water tray to form a cave and pour in water. Try to make a barrier with the rocks so that the water forms pools and caves.

What to do
Read the story about the little mermaid to the children and discuss it together. Using the story as a starting point, let the children play in small groups at the water tray with the rocks and the water. Gradually introduce some of the other play objects.

Don't impose your ideas but offer suggestions to further develop story-lines which should emerge from the children's play.

If you notice a theme developing help the children to formulate ideas by posing questions. When they have ideas encourage them to provide sentences rather than random ideas to tell you about their story. If necessary put their thoughts into sentences yourself.

As play develops offer a new element to their stories by introducing a new idea or item. Suggest a problem; 'The mermaid can't move and is trapped, how will you get her out?', or a surprise; 'When she came to the cave she found...'.

Questions to ask
What is happening? What are they doing? How did the mermaid save the man? How do you think she feels? Does the mermaid prefer it in the water or on land?

For younger children
An adult may need to help younger children to start off their play by demonstrating how some of the objects or people operate. Pretend that the mermaid is looking for a good place to live and ask the children if they can find one for her. Ask specific questions for them to solve.

For older children
Create some more scenarios, introduce a boat into the scene, or remove the treasure box for example. Encourage them to tell you a sequence of events which has happened.

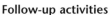

Follow-up activities
● Act out the stories in the role-play area with appropriate props.
● Make sea-sounds using sand on a lid by gently swishing it back and forth.
● Read seaside poems such as 'Ten little swimming crabs' by Beverley Randell (Nelson) and 'Don't be frightened Mr Octopus' by Malcolm Carrick in *All Sorts of Everything* (Heinemann).

OUT AND ABOUT

Learning objective
To listen to a story, and to use a growing vocabulary to express thoughts and feelings in response to the story.

Group size
Solitary play or small groups of two to four children.

What you need
A cement mixing tray of 1.5m diameter, selection of pebbles and rocks, play people and small boats, small plastic bear, selection of twigs and leaves, small containers, *Sailor Bear,* Martin Waddell (Walker Books).

Setting up
Place the tray on the table and use the rocks and pebbles to create an area like a boating lake, a harbour or a beach. Complete the scene with twigs and leaves. Pour some water carefully in to the tray to create some shallow pools.

What to do
Read the story of *Sailor Bear* to the whole group of children. Talk together about the story and encourage the children to identify with the bear. Ask them to think how he might have felt when his boat was in the rough water and also when he found a friend. Encourage the children to tell you their thoughts about the little bear's emotions.

Once the children are familiar with the story let them work at the tray either individually or in small groups using the toy bear, the boats and the people to re-enact the story for themselves.

Questions to ask
Have you ever felt lonely or frightened? Reinforce the sequence of events by asking: What happened when the bear decided to get a boat? When he found the sea was so big? When he sailed in the park? What did he do next? What would you do? Encourage the use of descriptive language through observation of detail, ask: Are all boats the same? What else have you seen that is the same colour blue as the boat?

For younger children
Encourage the children to take on the role of the bear and to say what they are doing and what is happening to them, as they do it! Help by providing any new vocabulary which the children need such as: harbour, cliffs or sailing boat.

For older children
Ask older children to explain to you, or to other children, what they are doing as they act out their stories in the tray. Encourage them to develop the storyline with their own ideas or to make up a completely new sequence of events for the bear. They may like to write down their new stories or they could tell you their ideas and you could scribe it for them.

Follow-up activities
● Make a large wall picture of the harbour scene together using paints or collage materials.
● Record the children's new story ideas on audio tape or key them in on the computer.

THE LAUNDRETTE

Learning objective
To role-play a familiar situation to encourage verbal skills.

Group size
Up to eight children.

What you need
Two large cardboard boxes, adhesive, scissors, paint, card for signs and labels, felt-tipped pens, pads and pencils, box of coins, empty detergent boxes (rinsed), overalls, laundry bags, baskets, clothes and sheets.

Setting up
Make the two large boxes in to a 'washing machine' and a 'tumble dryer'. Cut out a big circle shape from the side of the 'washer' and the 'dryer' to load the clothes into. Mark on dials, numbers, timer and coin slots. Provide a seating area nearby.

What to do
If you have a real washing machine at your location let the children watch the process. If not, talk together about what the children know from watching their parents use a washing machine at home or at the laundrette.

Let the children help you to set up the laundrette by positioning the equipment and arranging the chairs as a seated area. Discuss together what will be needed and how best to arrange it. Make large labels saying 'wash' and 'dry' for the two machines, make up a price list, and 'rules' along with an open/closed sign.

Play alongside the children and help sustain it by introducing a problem such as: a customer has lost a sock; one of the machines won't work; you don't have the right change.

Questions to ask
Why do we need to wash our clothes? What do you do when you go to a laundrette? Why do you need coins? What happens if you don't have a machine?

For younger children
Sort the clothes with similar sounding names, for example: a shirt, a skirt and a sheet, or pants, pullover and pillow case! Can they distinguish clearly between the words? Match this activity to the children's ability.

For older children
Let older children work together to fold the washing. Can two children fold a sheet together, folding in from top to bottom and edge to edge? Let them fold all the washing carefully to put into the laundry bags.

Follow-up activities
● Mime actions of simple household tasks and ask 'what am I doing?'.
● Read *Little old Mrs Pepperpot* by Alf Proysen (Beaver Books), discuss how hard it is to do jobs if you are very small.

THE HAIRDRESSER'S

Learning objective
To use role-play as a
basis for encouraging
verbal skills and
emergent writing.

Group size
Up to six children.

What you need
Water container (baby bath or washing-up bowl), table and small chairs, water sprays, towels, selection of different sized hair rollers, combs and brushes. A plastic toolbox is useful to contain these items. A mirror, empty shampoo bottles, ribbons, slides and covered elastic bands, wigs (if possible). Glossy magazines, toy telephone, appointment book, price list. Pretend hairdryer, dolls whose hair can be wetted, mop and bucket!

Setting up
Arrange the water tray at a suitable height for the children to work at while seated. Hang the mirror up and arrange the hairdressing items close by. Set up a table with the appointment book and telephone.

What to do
Start by talking together about previous visits the children may have made to the hairdresser's. Explain that you are going to provide a hairdresser's for the dolls. Show them how to make appointments by 'writing' the names in the book and then crossing them out when the client arrives. Discuss the price list and what kinds of styling are on offer in the salon.

Take one of the dolls and show the children what to do, by placing a towel around the dolls shoulders. Talk through the sequence of actions - washing, combing, drying and styling.

Let the children work together to act out the various functions and only intervene when necessary.

Questions to ask
Why do we wash our hair? What would happen if we didn't? Why do people go to the hairdresser's? Where do you wash your hair?

For younger children
Younger children will enjoy washing the doll's hair and may well immerse the whole doll! Encourage them to talk to the doll as they wash it. Some children will find brushing through the doll's hair very therapeutic.

For older children
Encourage older children to try more decorative hair-styles, using the rollers which requires quite complex manipulative skills. Let some children take messages and fill in the appointments book as this will be very useful to encourage emergent writing.

Follow-up activities
● Use the photocopiable sheet on page 59 where the children can complete the hair-styles and details on the pictures.
● Discuss and look at pictures of hair-styles from other cultures such as beading, plaiting and shaved heads.
● Set up the mirror so that individual children can draw or paint a self-portrait. Look at details and talk about face shape, eye colour and hair.

Develop the children's counting and number recognition skills using familiar and traditional rhymes, such as 'five little speckled frogs'. Use floating ice-cubes to help shape recognition and hold a tea-party to reinforce the concept of one-to-one correspondence!

TEN GREEN BOTTLES

Learning objective
To use numbers to ten in a familiar song, learning about the functions of addition and subtraction.

Group size
Ten children.

What you need
Ten small plastic lemonade bottles (same size). Green food colouring, strong piece of string the length of the water tray. Clearly written numbers 1-10 in a number line strip (optional).

Setting up
Fill a water tray. Add the green food colouring. Write numbers 1–10 on to the plastic bottles. Put the bottles in a container near the tray.

What to do
Allow the children to each collect a bottle and to fill it with the green water from the water tray. They may want to experiment by pouring and filling their bottles initially, and this can be encouraged as it is a useful introduction to capacity. Ask the children how many bottles the group has, count the bottles together several times.

Sing the song 'Ten Green Bottles' together around the water tray. When a bottle 'falls' off the wall push it under the water and fill it up. At each stage ask the children how many bottles are left.

If you think it will be easier for the children to register the bottles visually, then tie them in a line on to the string stretched across the water tray.

Once you have finished singing the song, allow the children to play freely with the bottles and observe if the number concepts are being practised.

Follow-up activities
● Attach a strip of Velcro sticky tape on a wall/display near the tray and let the children literally fix the bottles 'on the wall' encouraging children to experience the physical operation itself in order to grasp the mathematical concept.
● Reinforce the activity by using ten cups and observe the children's behaviour, encourage them to count out.
● Use the photocopiable sheet on page 60 to reinforce one-to-one correspondence and shape recognition.

Questions to ask
How many bottles are there now? If we add one – how many? How many bottles were there in the song? What happened to them? How many were left?

For younger children
Limit the song and group size to five. Large cut out plastic numbers may help to reinforce the numbers. Encourage the children to use their fingers on the surface of the water to try and write a number.

For older children
Introduce the number line and look at the order of the numbers, ask what goes before and after a certain number. Ask the children to take it in turns individually to count out an amount of bottles from the tray and to fill them up. Ask the children to show you how many bottles they have by holding up the relevant number of fingers.

STEPPING STONES

Learning objective
To explore the concept of relative size using natural materials.

Group size
Up to four children.

What you need
A water tray made of strong plastic, a collection of smooth pebbles and small boulders, small plastic model people (LEGO or similar).

Setting up
The children should help you set up, as they will benefit from the practical use of the resources. Collect everything together and put a small amount of water in the water tray. Put the pebbles in a box or container nearby and the people in another container.

What to do
Allow the children to handle and explore the pebbles. Listen carefully to what is being said. Intervene with questions to explore the concept of size. Which is the biggest? What shape is it?

Once the children have examined the stones carefully and told you all about them, ask if they know what a stepping stone is. Tell them that the play people need to get across the water without stepping in it and challenge the children to make a set of stepping stones the same size.

Let the children work in pairs and encourage them to discuss their selection of pebbles aloud.

Questions to ask
Where is the biggest stone? Where is the smallest? Can you sort the stones into sizes? Could you put the stones in a line starting with the biggest and going down to the smallest? Where will you put the stones in order to get the people across? How many stepping stones did you need?

For younger children
Select stones and pebbles that are more distinct in size. Tell the children to draw around the first pebble they select and to use it as a guide to place the next one on top. Is it the same size?

For older children
They may include other attributes such as weight as they feel the stones. When they select their stones they may choose stones which are similar in weight rather than size. Question them and determine which they mean. Extend the problem solving by asking if you used bigger stones would you need more or less? Why?

Follow-up activities
● Draw round the stones and record the size group they belong to.
● Make comparisons: 'This stone is the same size as ......'.
● Make a bridge with the stones as supports.

SHAPE IT

Learning objective
To know and recognise different shapes and be able to relate them to everyday objects.

Group size
Small groups around a large water tray; pairs or individuals around small trays.

What you need
Water tray, a collection of plastic ice-cube containers, plastic tubs, jelly moulds. Frozen coloured iced water in a variety of containers.

Setting up
Float the empty plastic containers on the surface of the water in the water tray. Push some ice shapes out and let them float too.

What to do
Tell the children they have to match the containers with the frozen ice shapes. Can they find which ice shape would fit back into which container? Look at the shapes of the plastic containers and ask if a child can show you which is a square, a circle and so on. Repeat the names of all the shapes until you are confident that the children can recognise them.

Allow the children to hold and look at the ice shapes and tell them to watch the colours to see what happens. Remind them not to hold each piece of ice too long or they will burn their fingers. As the ice starts to melt the shapes will be more difficult to distinguish so encourage them to work quickly!

Questions to ask
What shapes can you see in the water tray? Where do they come from? Which shape fits which container? What is your favourite shape? Why? What else do you know that is the same shape? What happens to the water when we pour it into the shape?

For younger children
Place other shapes such as those from a 'shape sorter' in the water for the children to play with to provide an introduction to shapes and their names.

For older children
Once the children have learned and can recognise regular shapes such as circle, square, triangle and rectangle introduce a greater variety of shapes.

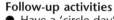

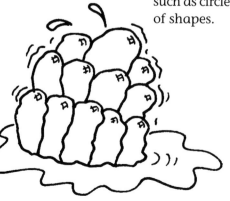

> **Follow-up activities**
> ● Have a 'circle day' or a 'square morning'. Ask the children to bring in things in the relevant shape for a display.
> ● Go for a 'shape walk'. Ask the children to draw or collect artefacts in a particular shape.
> ● Collect natural objects and manufactured objects related to one shape. Do the children make reference to the specific shape?

DUCKS

Learning objective
To understand the
mathematical concepts
of addition and
subtraction using a set
of objects.

Group size
Five children.

What you need
Water tray, five plastic ducks of the same or similar size, blue food colouring, leaves to float on the water, pebbles.

Setting up
Put the pebbles or stones in the bottom of the tray. Fill with water and add some blue colouring. Float the leaves on the surface. Line the ducks up ready, out of the water.

What to do
Introduce the children to 'the pond' and explain that today the ducks are going swimming. Ask the children to line up the ducks and to count them. Let each child place one duck in to the pond and count them as they go in.

Sing the rhyme 'Five little ducks went swimming one day':
'Five little ducks went swimming one day,
over the hill and far away,
Mother duck called "quack quack come back"
but only four little ducks came swimming
back...'.
(Repeat and subtract one each time.)

Let the children move the ducks around the pond and take it in turns to remove one duck each time the rhyme requires it.

Questions to ask
Where are the ducks? How many can you count? Will they float on the pond? Let's count them as they get in. If I add one more, how many are there now? If two hid away, how many ducks are left?

For younger children
You could provide number tags on square card with string to fix around the ducks' necks to identify them as specific numbers, to help younger children to count.

For older children
Provide a variety of different sized and coloured ducks to increase the possibilities for children to place them in order or in to sets. Provide a larger duck to be 'mother'!

Follow-up activities
● Use finger puppets to sing this rhyme.
● Make a collection of rhymes directly linked to the number five, such as 'Five in the bed' and 'Five currant buns'.

TEA PARTY

Learning objective
*To match one-to-one,
to identify sets of items.*

Group size
Four children.

What you need
A water tray, water, a squirt of mild washing-up liquid, a washing mop or similar. Plastic tea-set including cups, saucers, plates, teapot and jug in a variety of different colours.

Setting up
Put the water, washing-up liquid and the mop in the tray ready for 'washing up time'. Mix up the tea-set components either in the water or at the side of the tray.

What to do
Let the children start by free play with the tea-set in the water, pretending to wash up. Then introduce the idea of each child collecting their own set of objects. The obvious set to start with is colour, so allocate a particular child a specific colour and ask them to collect everything from the tea-set that they can in that colour. Hold up a cup, for example, and ask the child to find something that goes with it and so on. Encourage the children to compile their own tea-sets at the side of the tray in their chosen colour.

Next make sets of, for example, cups. Ask a child if they can make a set of cups (in any colour) and then of plates. Make as many different types of sets as possible, depending on the items you have available and encourage the children to count up the items in their sets when they have finished.

Questions to ask
What shall we put with this plate? What do you think goes with this red cup? Do you think we can put this blue saucer with this blue jug? If the children are able to make a link between two items encourage them to do so (it may be 'we eat off them' for both small and large plates for instance). Where do you keep these things in your house?

Follow-up activities
● Provide further matching one-to-one activities – straws to bottles, socks to shoes for example.
● Make up a picnic basket for the 'Three Bears'. Tell the children they must match up the cups and plates to the relevant bears (for baby, mummy and daddy) sorting by size.
● Use plastic crockery and cutlery and ask the children to set place settings at the table, making sure there is one set of items for each place.

For younger children
Encourage younger children to match items one-to-one. You could place a row of saucers down and ask a child to find a cup to match each one. Set out the cups and saucers side by side, and ask if there are the same number of cups as saucers: how can we check? If the children are not sure ask them to match them up by putting the cups on to the saucers.

For older children
Look for different ways of making sets. The objects in the sets may have the same features, for example, they are the same shape or the same size. Some children will be able to consider more than one feature at the same time; the set they make may be all red and all cups.

FIVE SPECKLED FROGS

Learning objective
To understand addition and subtraction through a practical task.

Group size
Five children.

What you need
Five plastic frogs (obtained from a toy shop/educational suppliers), green food colouring, an old log, twigs, leaves, pebbles or stones.

Setting up
Place the log in the tray and make sure it is secure and does not rock – it may need two pebbles or stones to secure it. Pour water into the tray so that it is half way up the log. Put in some drops of green food colouring and mix it up evenly in the water. Place some leaves to float on the water and position the five frogs on their log.

What to do
Ask the children: how many frogs are sitting on the log? Take all the frogs off the log and invite the children to put the frogs back on, counting them in turn.

Remove each frog in turn again and ask the children how many are left each time one is removed.

Sing the song 'Five little speckled frogs':
'Five little speckled frogs, sat on a speckled log,
Eating a most delicious lunch (yum, yum),
One jumped into the pool where it was nice and cool,
Then there were four green speckled frogs!' (Count down each time.)

Questions to ask
How many? How do you know? (Encourage the children to practise counting and checking rather than guessing). If two frogs went off for a swim how many would there be? Introduce some simple subtraction scenarios, then let the children try them out.

Follow-up activities
● Use another set of animal objects, for example, pigs from the farm or plastic spiders, to see if the children can carry out the same task in a new context.
● Ask how many leaves are in the tray? How many twigs? Encourage the children to count objects whenever possible as a natural part of their play.
● Use a small hand net to 'catch' things which you have floated on the water and then ask the children to count and sort them.

For younger children
These children may need to see the numbers written down and to see the frogs in a line to visualise the number and the amount.

For older children
Provide counting reinforcement by introducing some simple problem solving. What if three frogs went under the log? (Let the children try it.) How many are left? Add extra frogs to observe if the children are counting and checking accurately.

SEAWORLD

Learning objective
To practise addition and counting.

Group size
Maximum of four.

What you need
A water tray, bowl or low sink, blue or green food colouring, plastic fishes which could be marked with numerals or an appropriate number of dots (depending on the level of the child) using a water-proof ink pen, a small fishing net for each child, leaves, ferns (optional). Some reference books about fish.

Setting up
Add blue or green colouring to the water in the water tray, to represent a lake or a river, float leaves on the surface. Place the plastic fish into the water and make sure they are spaced out. Display a picture of a pond or a lake nearby to stimulate the activity.

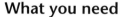

What to do
Introduce the activity by singing the rhyme 'One, two, three, four, five once I caught a fish alive' with the children. Encourage the children to role-play fishing in the tray.

Give each child their own net and allow them to practise scooping and catching with it. Now challenge the children to catch and count the fish. Encourage further mathematical language such as more than and fewer than, as the children 'fish'.

Questions to ask
Who lives in the sea? Where? Do they live on the top or underneath? Why do they live under the water? How many fish are you going to catch? How many fish have you caught? Who has caught the most fish? Who has the least? What number is on the fish? Have you seen that number anywhere else?

For younger children
Young children may be pre-occupied with scooping the net in the water and will happily spend a lot of time splashing and moving the water around. This is not a waste of time however as it will develop hand and eye co-ordination skills.

For older children
Play fishing games, by using magnets and metal clips attached to the fish. If the fishes are marked with numbers or dots the children could add the numbers together. Once all the fish have been caught they could add up all the numbers to see who has the most. The children will need to have developed their hand and eye skills in order to connect and catch the fish.

Follow-up activities
● Set up the home corner as a 'fish and chip shop'.
● Use a large cardboard box (big enough for the children to get in) as a boat, let them dress up in macs and wellies and with a 'fishing rod', send them to sea.
● Visit a fishmonger's stall or a fish department of a supermarket. Look at the wide variety of fish, see how they are laid out on ice.
● Make, paint and model different fish.

MARVELLOUS MIXTURES

Learning objective
*To practise measuring
and to learn about
capacity.*

Group size
*Four to six children
around a water tray.*

What you need
A collection of plastic bottles of various sizes (some with lids), jugs,
food colourings, pipettes or simple plastic syringes.

Setting up
Fill the water tray. Put out the resources listed above.

What to do
Show the children how to put droplets of neat food colouring into
bottles using the pipettes or syringes and then to add water and put
the lids on. Let them observe the effects of the food colouring, giving
the bottles a shake to mix it up well.

Allow the children to float their bottles on the water in the water
tray. Let them open up their bottles and pour and mix the colours in
the water tray.

Use the spoons and jugs to pour and measure. Encourage the
children to transfer water to the different containers.

Questions to ask
What is in your bottle? What is it for? Can you pour it out carefully,
or measure it out in spoonfuls?

For younger children
Allow free play pouring and mixing and include other familiar props
if necessary such as tea cups and beakers. Use terms with younger
children such as 'full' or 'half full' rather than exact measurements.

For older children
Use more advanced measurement language such as
'more than ...', or 'less than...'. Use measuring jugs
with levels marked and ask the children to
fill to a certain level.

Follow-up activities
● Introduce plastic
tubing in the water
tray for filling up
vessels.
● Use kitchen
measuring spoons
with specific
measures marked for
pretend play.
● Make a chemist's
shop in the home
corner with your
marvellous mixtures
on sale.

The eight activities in this chapter provide ways of using water play to develop the children's personal and social skills. Caring for pets, considering personal hygiene and understanding the importance of caring for our world and each other are topics covered in this chapter.

BATHTIME

Learning objective
To develop an understanding of the importance of personal hygiene.

Group size
Small group of three to four children.

What you need
A selection of brushes: toothbrush, nailbrush, a backbrush and a sponge. A variety of soaps. A baby bath, half filled with warm water. Towels, talcum powder, comb, dolls (include a boy doll and one which is really grubby!).

Setting up
Position the half-filled bath ready and have the equipment to hand.

What to do
Show the children the grubby doll. Ask them: what can we do with her? Talk about how the children wash themselves at home. Some children may bath and some may shower. Do they bath before bedtime or in the morning; with a brother or sister, or by themselves? Encourage them to talk about 'bath time' at home. Do they have bubbles or play with toys? Be sensitive to different cultures and individual family routines.

Reinforce the need to wash hands at particular times such as, before meals and after going to the toilet.

Let the children demonstrate how to wash using the grubby doll and the soaps and brushes and ask them to talk about what they are doing. Increase the children's vocabulary of body parts, by making particular observations: look she has dirty knees, you will need to wash the doll's tummy or elbow. They can finish by carefully drying the doll, using the talcum powder and combing her hair.

Follow-up activities
● Arrange a visit from a mother and her baby and let her show how she bathes the baby.
● Look at how different animals wash themselves. If possible observe birds bathing in a bird bath or puddles.
● Look at different materials to see which ones are the best for drying the wet dolls.
● Play 'Simon Says' to learn body parts.

Questions to ask
Why do we need to wash? What would it be like if we never washed? What do you feel like when you are dirty or sweaty? Can you see germs? How can we get rid of them?

For younger children
Show younger children how to follow a sequence to clean the doll: wash, rub with soap and water, rinse and dry. Demonstrate and do it alongside the children.

For older children
Experiment with soap and liquid soaps. Find out what happens if you leave a bar of soap in water overnight. What happens? Where has the soap gone? Let the children try cold and warm water. Does the temperature of the water make a difference?

DOLPHIN

Learning objective
To develop care and concern for living things.

Group size
A small group of four children.

What you need
Water tray, nets, plastic sea life animal set (include whales and dolphins), deep blue paint or food colouring, plastic food tubs, books about whales and dolphins, suitable videos such as *Free Willy* (Warner Home Video (UK) Limited), pencils, colouring pencils, paper and paints.

Setting up
Fill the water tray and add deep blue paint or colouring. Add the sea life animals. Put some of the dolphins in to the nets and the tubs.

What to do
Show the children some clips from the video showing the animals enjoying their natural environment.

Discuss with the children the sea creatures' needs and talk about how and where the dolphins play. Contrast this with what happens when they are trapped in fishing nets or kept in captivity.

Allow the children to enjoy free play with the whales and dolphins in the water and encourage them to let the creatures 'enjoy' the water.

Questions to ask
Where do whales and dolphins live? Have the children ever seen any real ones? How big are they? Would they fit into this room? What happens to the fish when they are trapped and tangled in the nets? How do you think they feel when they are trapped or kept in small pools? How can you lift a whale out of the pool and take it to the sea? Where do you like to play? Outside, in the park or shut in a very small place? Do you like to play with other children?

For younger children
Younger children will enjoy playing with the creatures in the water. Help them to mime swimming actions, show them how to use their hands and wrists without jerking and splashing.

For older children
Let older children experiment to find ways of lifting the whales and dolphins out of the tray. Afterwards ask them to draw their designs.

Follow-up activities
● Music and movement – use arms and hands to express the movement of the large animals and fish in the sea.
● Contact organisations such as 'International Dolphin Watch' (Telephone: 01482 631378) to learn more about dolphins.
● Read *Dilo and the call of the deep* by Horace Dobbs (WATCH Publishing), the story of a baby dolphin. (Suitable to read in short extracts to your older children.)

SOS

Learning objective
To learn to treat living creatures and the environment with care and concern.

Group size
Individual, pairs or small group.

What you need
Water container, cooking oil, black paint, paper towels, liquid detergent, soap, nail brush, warm water, a set of sea world animals, aprons.

Setting up
Mix the paint and oil and add to the water in the water tray. Place the plastic animals in to the tray and allow them to become covered in the oil slick. Make sure the children wear aprons.

What to do
Let the children discover the toys in the 'oil slick'. Talk to them about how sometimes animals, especially birds, get covered in oil when there is a spillage. Explain to them how dangerous this is for wildlife, and how important it is to rescue them and clean them straight away. Tell the children that the toys need to be cleaned and made comfortable.

Provide the detergent and nail brush and let the children decide how they will clean the animals. Observe how they approach the task. What do they choose to use? How do they work together?

Questions to ask
What has happened to the toys? How has it happened? How do the toys feel? What do they look like? What can we do to make them feel better? How can you clean them?

For younger children
Advise younger children on how to clean the animals and start them off if necessary. Encourage them to speak to the animals: do they comfort them with cuddles or tell them off for being dirty?

For older children
Let them set up a rescue centre for the animals. Encourage them to decide how to approach it and observe what sort of things they think the animals will need.

Follow-up activities
● Look for different ways to get rid of oil, which is the best way?
● Draw on paper with a black wax crayon. Colour the picture in and then dab the black wax pattern with cooking oil. The coloured section will become transparent.
● Discuss the need to be careful in disposing with rubbish, cans and plastic bags with regard to damage to wildlife.
● Observe birds bathing, eating and flying.

SEA HARVEST

Learning objective
To learn that fish is a food of the sea and that all living creatures are part of the natural world on which we rely.

Group size
Four children.

What you need
A collection of plastic fish from a toy shop/educational suppliers, bean netting cut into a piece that will fit into the water tray, blue food colouring (optional), small dipper nets.

Setting up
Fill the water tray and add the food colouring if required. Put the fish in the water, and place the netting at the side of the tray.

What to do
Explain to the children that at harvest time we collect in crops such as wheat and fruit and vegetables from the land. Tell them that there is a harvest time in the sea too. Let the children look at all the fish in the water. Give them time to see where they all are and to count them. Suggest to the children that they can work together to collect up the fish.

Encourage them to work out how they can all help and share the task of collecting the fish together. Once they have collected all the fish in the net they will have to haul the net in together. This is very much a team activity, and as an adult observing you may need to intervene as some children will find this difficult.

Questions to ask
Where do you buy the fish you eat? Where do the shops get the fish? Would you like to go out to sea in a boat to catch fish? Do you like fish? Is it a hard job to catch fish?

For younger children
Use larger fish and nets for younger children so that they can physically cope with the task. Encourage them to work in pairs as they may find working in a larger group difficult.

For older children
Encourage group work with older children and observe how well they work together. Repeat the exercise with single sex groups and see if the co-operation outcome differs from a mixed group.

Follow-up activities
● Visit a fishmonger's to look at real fresh fish, use all the senses to explore them.
● Make the home corner into a fishmonger's for imaginative play, or make a boat from a box, dress up like fishermen and catch fish.
● Use the photocopiable sheet on page 61 to practise counting skills.

GOLDFISH

Learning objective
To learn how to take responsibility in caring for a pet.

Group size
Individual tasks with whole group involvement.

What you need
A glass or a tank to hold the fish, (not a round goldfish bowl), goldfish (appropriate to the size of your tank), a small fishing net and a plastic scraper, rocks, stones, gravel or sand, some aquatic plants and suitable food. Books about goldfish.

Setting up
Show the empty tank to the children. Talk about the goldfish and explain that you need to get a new home ready before they arrive. Select the best site for the tank out of direct sunlight, on a firm base where the children can see and reach it.

Clean the stones, rocks and gravel before you put them in the tank. Fill another container with tap water and let it stand for two days to allow the chlorine smell to disperse. Pour the water gently into the tank. Put a sheet of paper on top of the gravel to prevent it being disturbed. The paper will float to the surface and is easily removed. Keep some of the water to top up the tank later.

What to do
Talk about what the fish will need to live happily. Explain that you will need to take care of them by feeding them and keeping the tank clean. Establish a feeding routine and let the children take turns. Make a pictorial chart to show what they must do to take care of the fish and display it for reference near the tank.

Questions to ask
Does anyone have goldfish at home? What do we need to take care of them properly? How can we find out? What would happen if we did not care for them or gave them the wrong food? What would happen if the fish got out of the tank? How can we get some water into the tank?

For younger children
Make sure the children understand that it is not good to overfeed the fish. Let them measure out a small amount and give to the fish at a regular time each day.

For older children
Let the children take turns at cleaning the tank as well as feeding. It requires skill to locate and remove scraps from the tank. The children can practise in the water tray to find different ways of picking up small objects. Make sure they wash their hands afterwards.

Follow-up activities
● Prepare a large book as a Group Diary. Let the children add pictures, comments and photos about the fish.
● Look at other water creatures such as tadpoles, frogs.
● Make goldfish mobiles from orange Cellophane and hang them so they move in the breeze.

PIRATE'S PANIC

Learning objective
To work in a group to solve a problem involving personal and social decisions.

Group size
Four children.

What you need
A water tray or deep storage box, blue food colouring, a plastic boat, two to four plastic pirates, string, small bits of balsa wood, assortment of reclaimed materials.

Setting up
Fill the water tray and add the food colouring, for effect. Float the boat on the surface of the water, and place the two pirates on a surface near the water tray, put out the reclaimed materials and pieces of wood.

What to do
Begin by setting the scene. Tell the children that two pirates have been set adrift at sea in a small boat and they are looking for an island. Place two pirates in the small boat and tell the children that one leans too far out of the boat and falls out. At this point let the children put one of the pirates in the water and then ask them open-ended questions about what might happen to the pirate, what his friend would do and how he could help.

Encourage the children to think through the problem themselves and to consider how the pirate still in the boat would be feeling in that situation. The reclaimed materials and pieces of wood at the side of the water tray are designed to prompt the children and to provide strategies for solving the problem. Prevent them just reaching into the water and pulling the pirate out!

Ask the children to take turns with their ideas to prevent the session becoming disorganised and in order to make the best use of the suggestions and ideas contributed.

Questions to ask
Have you ever fallen in the water? How did you feel? How do you think the pirate in the water would feel? How would his friend in the boat have felt? How should you behave near water? What would be a good set of rules?

For younger children
Younger children will tend to focus on the physical problems of the pirate sinking and going underwater. They may need more support with problem solving, thinking how to go about it and what to do. Help by looking at the reclaimed materials and wood pieces at the side of the activity and saying: could these help us? What could we use these for?

For older children
Older children will be able to articulate their feelings better and so the value of talking and questioning is just as important as the physical retrieval of the pirate. Encourage the children to explore their own ideas however unusual they may be.

Follow-up activities
● Give children some other problem-solving opportunities. It may be difficult at first and the children will require significant adult intervention but as they become more able they will begin to ask for more challenges.
● Talk about the importance of learning to swim for your own safety. Set up a dolls swimming pool in the water tray, for imaginative play.
● Use the photocopiable sheet on page 62 to reinforce the activity.

GALA TIME

Learning objective
To recognise that taking part in an activity is important and how to deal appropriately with winning and losing.

Group size
At least four children.

What you need
A water tray, some lengths of string, some plastic or clockwork figures/ creatures, blue food colouring (optional), small card squares numbered '1,2,3,4' a whistle.

Setting up
The water tray is going to be the scene of a swimming gala. Fill the tray and add the food colouring if you wish. Make four lanes by putting lengths of string across the widest part of the tray and secure these with tape on each end. Tie some string around your figures, making sure it is long enough to reach across the tray with some spare. If you are using clockwork toys don't wind them up until you are ready to start. Decide who will blow the whistle and what they will say. Place a contender in each lane

What to do
Explain to the children that the water tray is going to be a swimming pool and that today it is gala or race day. Ask them to each select a lane and tell them that they will be the swimmer in that lane. Explain that it is a race and there will be a first, second, third and fourth. Talk about the winner and the loser.

Let the children have several turns so there are many races. Encourage the children to congratulate each other.

Questions to ask
What is a winner? What is a loser? What things are you good at? What are you not so good at? Can you tell me some famous winners and losers? What do you say to a winner or loser?

For younger children
A lot of adult support and a careful watching eye will be needed. Show younger children how to pull the figures through the water itself, so they play fairly.

For older children
Older children will be able to say who has won but make sure they watch to see who is second and third too. Suggest that one child be the judge and encourage them to run the whole 'gala'. Another child can be a starter and ask them to involve two more new children and to pass on the rules and procedures to them.

Follow-up activities
● Practise other games which involve turn-taking, decisions and rules.
● Change the scene to a boat race and play the same game with less competitors.
● Tell the story of the 'Hare and the tortoise' (*Aesop's Fables*). Encourage the children to make up their own version of the story with different characters.

GAME TIME

Learning objective
To use co-operation
skills to work in a small
group.

Group size
Small group; working
in pairs.

What you need
Large drinking straws, small balls (ideally table tennis) or boats, a water tray, string.

Setting up
Fill the water tray and then divide it up into two lanes using a piece of string stretched across the tray, and then taped down at the side. Use large straws and lightweight balls such as table tennis balls so that they will move easily across the water's surface.

What to do
Ask the children to get into pairs and to think of a team name. (This is optional.) Position two teams of children at the water tray, facing their team mate. Explain that the aim of the game is to blow the ball across the water to each other, and the team mate must then return it. Encourage them to work as a team and to work as efficiently as possible.

Questions to ask
How are your 'team' going to do this? What will you both need to remember? If you both blow at once will it be the best way? Why? Why do you need to share and work with each other?

For younger children
Younger children may find it difficult to work together. It may be better to divide the tray into four separate lanes so that the children can work independently but can still experience the feeling of being in a group and the considerations that this requires.

For older children
Try different types of teams with older children, for example, compare and contrast the way mixed gender pairs and single sex groups work. Try this activity using other objects to get across the water which will give the children the opportunity for problem solving.

Follow-up activities
● Tell some stories that involve getting across water such as *The Gingerbread Man* (Ladybird).
● Use the idea of a co-operative activity in outside-play asking children to work in pairs to achieve a specific goal.
● Ask children how they feel when they work together and ask them to record this through drawings and writing.

Ideas for exploring the world in which we live are provided in this chapter. Investigate the properties of water: how it moves and behaves, and how water reacts with other materials such as fabrics in the activities included here.

RAINBOW COLOURS

Learning objective
To experience the properties of materials by looking through things.

Group size
Whole group discussion and experiments; individual or paired investigation.

What you need
A selection of transparent containers (coloured and plain, clear plastic bottles with tops), a cup, old spectacles/sun glasses, Sellotape, scissors, cardboard tubes. Some of the following – inks, vegetable dyes, crêpe paper, sweet wrappers, Cellophane, polythene. Droppers, paints, paint brushes and paper, ice-cube moulds.

Setting up
Prepare some coloured ice-cubes in advance. Make viewers by covering one end of a tube with paper and attaching it firmly (provide transparent, opaque and translucent paper). Fill the plastic bottles with coloured water, using inks, dyes or paint and screw tops on securely. Cut some of the papers into squares.

What to do
Ask the children to look at objects around them using the sunglasses and the viewers which you have made and describe what they can see. Let them repeat the activity using several layers of coloured polythene. Can they tell you how different things look now? If the children use two different colours of paper what happens? Try using red and yellow for example - can the children see what colour they have produced?

Shake the liquids in the bottles and encourage the children to look through them at other objects too. Show the children how things look different when you look 'through' the liquids; can they tell you how?

Put the coloured ice-cubes into the water and watch them dissolve. Place the coloured papers into the water tray too.

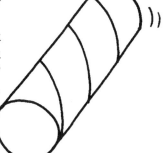

Questions to ask
What can you see when you look through the paper, the bottle, the viewer? If you put the bottle on its side how does the water look different? What do you think has happened to the water? Where has the colour gone from the ice-cubes and the papers? How can we make the colours lighter?

For younger children
Let them explore how they can change the depth of a colour by diluting with water. Make colour strips showing the different shades of colour.

For older children
Ask the children to draw a picture of the cup and then look at it through the liquid in the plastic bottle. Now ask them to draw another picture to show how it has changed.

Follow-up activities
● Look at reflections in mirrors, puddles and ponds. Make a display of shiny things. Look at patterns in kaleidoscopes.
● Find out about rainbows and the colours of the spectrum.
● Use vegetables such as onion skins, beetroot and blackberries to make your own dyes.

CROW'S PROBLEM

Learning objective
To explore the shape which water takes up and how objects replace water space.

Group size
Whole group for the story, then individually, in pairs or as a small group.

What you need
A copy of Aesop's fable 'The Crow and the Pitcher', containers (transparent and different shapes), a picture or a model of a crow, a bucket, coloured Sellotape, corks and pieces of wood. A collection of solid objects of various sizes such as a house brick, metal lids, metal spoons and coins.

Setting up
Fill the bucket to the brim. Arrange it on the water tray so that the children can see what is happening. Fill the containers, some half full, some almost to the top. Mark the water level with the tape.

What to do
Read the beginning of the story to the children. It tells the tale of a thirsty crow who finds a shallow pool but the water is too low for him to drink. He wants the water very badly and doesn't know what to do. Show the picture/model of a crow to the children and talk about the shape of his beak.

Ask the children for their ideas for how the crow could get to the water. Try out the children's ideas and the following experiments:
● Let the children place stones into the bucket and watch what happens. Take the stones out and refill the bucket each time a new group comes to experiment. Try with different objects including some that float.
● To show the same function put coins into the marked containers one by one and watch the water levels rise. Then take the coins out and watch the water level drop.

Finish reading the story of the crow to the children telling how he raised the water level by putting stones into the water.

Questions to ask
How can the crow reach the water? Why has some of the water spilled out? Is there more water now? Will it only work if you use stones? Which stones are best? How many coins can we put in before the water spills over the edge?

For younger children
Allow the children to play with different containers, filling and emptying them. Discuss with them how the water changes shape to fit the shape of its container.

Follow-up activities
● Make jellies in different shaped moulds. Make coloured ice-moulds to show how water takes on different shapes.
● Use the photocopiable sheet on page 63 to help the children sequence events from the story.
● Remind the children that animals need water. Make a bird-table with a bird-bath and water.

For older children
Using the marked containers can the children predict where the water will be if the containers are tilted? Try turning the containers upside down. Discuss what will happen.

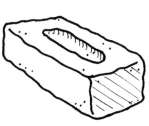

UP AND DOWN

Learning objective
To find out how to
make water move.

Group size
Pairs.

What you need
Vegetable dye, clear plastic tube, funnels, jug, two large plastic jars or
containers, a bucket and a block to stand it on. Water tray. (CARE!
Prepare a weak sterilising solution to wash the plastic tubes.)

Setting up
Place the bucket on the block in the water tray. Fill it with water.
Place some containers as obstacles in the water tray and drape the
tube over them. Prepare some coloured water in a jug. Fix funnels at
either end of the plastic tube.

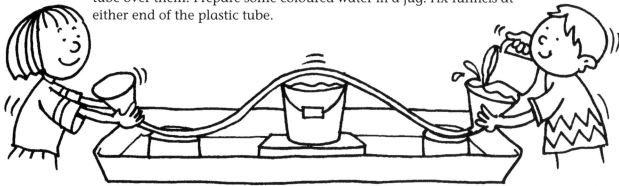

What to do
Show the children how to fill the tube with water and to move the water
from the bucket over the jars and into the bottom of the tray. Ask the
children to work in pairs holding opposite ends of the tube. They
need to take turns to move the water by tipping and tilting the tube
to watch the coloured water flow through the tube. Once they have
experienced the way the water flows encourage them to experiment
by putting different objects in the tray as a sort of obstacle course.

Questions to ask
Will the water go over any obstacle? Can you make it go over really
high things? What will happen if you move the pipe/jars up or down?
Why do you think you need to put your finger over the end. What
happens if you do not?

For younger children
Younger children will find it hard to work with a partner for this
activity. Pair these children with an adult who can guide their
movements and help them to control the equipment.

For older children
Place two jars at different levels, each one half full of water. Using the
plastic tube demonstrate how to suck the water gently through the tube.
When the water fills the tube tell the child to put a finger over the bottom
end. Place the tube well into the water of the bottom jar. Release their
finger and watch the water flow. Let the children try to move water in
this way. Move the jars up and down. Does it make a difference?

Follow-up activities
● Talk about how
water moves around
the house – showers,
sinks, toilets. Where
does it come from?
● Use guttering and
plumber's pipes to
move water up,
down and around.
● Make a 'water
world' environment
for some play people,
with water slides and
chutes.

MOP IT UP

Learning objective
To explore the properties of materials, observing similarities and differences.

Group size
Four to six children with an adult.

What you need
A variety of fabrics (include some waterproof and some plastics), some commercially made mopping cloths/sponge, food colouring or coloured inks, an eye dropper.

Setting up
Cut up the fabric pieces so that they are all the same size and shape. Put the food colouring into saucers.

What to do
Set the activity in the context of spring cleaning. Tell the children you are trying to find which is the best fabric to use to clean and mop up the play house. Explain that the fabric must be good at soaking up water.

Place three different pieces of fabric on the table, and let the children handle the fabric and talk about how each one feels. Ask them to decide which of the fabrics would make the best mop.

Using the dropper put a similar amount of water onto each piece. The fabric may change colour or even stain once it is wet. Some fabrics will absorb water faster than others. Let the children experiment with the rest of the fabrics.

Questions to ask
What happened to the drop of water? Where has the water gone? (It may be on the top in droplet form, stay in the fabric or go all the way through.) If we spilt the water what would be the best thing to use as a mop? How can you find out? What happens if the fabric gets 'full' of water? What should we do?

Follow-up activities
● Use shaped sponges for printing.
● Tie-dye fabrics. Show how the wet dye will not reach the tied parts of the fabric.
● Make wax resistant pictures to show how to stop water soaking into the paper.

For younger children
Give them each a strip of blotting paper or a tissue. Put some coloured water in a saucer and tell them to dip one end of the blotting paper into the colour puddle. Let them watch the colour run up the strip.

For older children
Let the children experiment to find out which is the most absorbent paper (from a selection including foil, shiny, blotting, coffee filter paper, tissue, Cellophane and crêpe). Observe how they approach the task. Do they copy what you did with the fabrics or try something different?

SPRAYS

Learning objective
To explore how water behaves, to examine water pressure.

Group size
Small groups with an adult.

What you need
Plastic bottles, polythene bags. Small world houses and buildings. Some objects that will float.

Setting up
Make holes in the plastic bottles using a hot knitting needle. (CARE! An adult must do this.) Vary the height and position of the holes, some all the way around, in spirals going up and down around the sides or at random, and make some small holes and some large ones. Use some transparent bottles so that the children can see the water level. Do the same with the plastic bags. Fill the water tray. Protect the floor with a suitable covering.

What to do
Put the bottles and bags in the tray and let the children investigate how the water sprays. Ask the children to predict which holes the water will come out of, before they squeeze. Show them how to fill the bags with water and how to squeeze the water out through the holes. Show them how the spray varies depending on how it is held and squeezed.

After the children have enjoyed their investigation for a while extend the play by adding play houses into the water tray. Tell the children to pretend that the houses are on fire, and ask if the children can aim their sprays at the houses to put out the fire.

Questions to ask
Which hole will the water come out of first? Does more water make the spray go further? How can you stop the water coming out of the holes? How can you make your spray reach the houses?

For younger children
Let younger children enjoy the physical process of feeling the water through their fingers. Encourage the children to describe what is happening, develop their vocabulary to include squirt, spray, sprinkle, jet and gush.

For older children
Ask the children to use the sprays and jets to push objects under the water. Can they use the spray to move things along in the water?

Follow-up activities
● Design a watering can. Decide if the spray has to be fine, fast, big, or wide.
● Link the activity with discussion about jets and fountains. Can the children find a way to make water spray upwards or outwards?
● Role-play fire-fighting outside. Provide helmets, hoses and buckets.

BUBBLES

Learning objective
To experience the
properties of water, to
investigate surface
tension.

Group size
Up to ten children.

What you need
Florist's wire, plastic cups, a large shallow tray, straws, paints, washing-up liquid, glycerine, label and pen.

Setting up
Make up solutions of washing-up liquid, a little water and paint. Make strong colour mixes. Mix different strength solutions using the washing-up liquid, glycerine and a small quantity of water. Put into cups and label. Leave to one side.

What to do
Show the children how to blow through a straw into the mixture to make bubbles. Keep on blowing until the bubbles rise up and foam over the sides. (CARE! Stress that the children must not suck the mixture up the straws.)
Show the children how to twist the wire to form the bubble catcher and how to skim the surface of the water to pick up a bubble.
Emphasise the vocabulary: transparent, reflection, burst or pop. Ask the children to describe the colours and the rainbow effect.

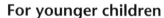

Questions to ask
How is the bubble made? What shape is the bubble? Does it matter how hard you blow? Why do the bubbles burst? Can you see through the bubble? What do things look like through the bubble? Where do you think the bubble goes when it is popped?

For younger children
Show the children how to capture the bubbles by gently placing a piece of paper on top of them. Roll the paper over the bubbles rather than press it, and the bubbles will be transferred onto the paper. Use different colours to make multi-coloured prints.

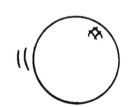

For older children
Use the clear bubble solution and wire. Scoop the solution onto the wire and blow. See who can make the biggest bubble. Encourage them to try the different strengths of bubble solution and to decide which one works best.

Follow-up activities
● Link with work on rainbows.
● Talk about going on an imaginary journey in a bubble. Where might you go?
● Find other ways of making bubbles: use a whisk with bubble bath solution; try shaking mixtures in a bottle.

THE BOAT RACE

Learning objective
To find out about the special properties of magnets.

Group size
Four children, two each side of the tray.

What you need
Plastic storage box, two blocks or bricks, strong magnets taped to rulers (one for each child playing), corks and dressmaker pins, paper-clips, drawing pins and triangles of paper.

Setting up
Arrange the box so that it is suspended between the blocks/bricks. Stand the box in a larger tray, surround it with wads of newspaper and fill it with water. Make cork boats by fixing the paper triangles with dressmaker pins to form a sail. Attach the paper-clip to the bottom of the 'boat' with the drawing pin.

What to do
Show the magnets to the children. They may already be familiar with decorative magnets. Tell them that the ends of the magnets are called poles and that one is S pole and one is N pole. Explain that S and N will pull towards each other but that two Ns or two Ss push each other away.

Give the children time for free play with the magnets, and watch them putting the ends together and feeling the pull. Let them see how the magnet will pull other metal too as well as another magnet.

When they are ready, position the children either side of the tray and show them how to hold the magnet underneath the water tray to move the boats. Let the children each choose a boat and they can try to control their boat using the magnet attached to the ruler. When they have acquired some control, introduce obstacles in the water for them to manoeuvre their boats around.

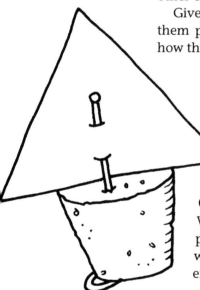

Questions to ask
Will magnets pull everything? What sort of things can they pull? Do you think the magnet will be able to work through water? How can we make the boats move? Does it matter which end of the ruler (magnet) you use?

For younger children
Let the children try to pull their boats down to the bottom. Try different ways of doing this by putting more pins onto the boat or reducing the amount of water. They will need a strong magnet to make it work.

For older children
Will magnets work through other materials? Let older children go around the room and try through glass, paper, wood. Collect the things that work well and label them.

Follow-up activities
● Look at different types of boats and talk about how they move.
● Design a game, such as the pathway for a bee going to a hive. Make a bee out of Plasticine and fix a paper-clip to the base. Let the children try to move the bee across the card using magnets.
● Make a collection of metal objects and investigate which ones are attracted by a magnet.

CROCODILE WORLD

Learning objective
To explore features of the natural world, floating and sinking.

Group size
Small group.

What you need
Plastic crocodiles, water, green food colouring, plants, rocks, pebbles, leaves, twigs and string. Waterproof tray with a plastic sheet underneath. Samples of different materials (paper, plastic, wool, card and wood).

Setting up
Start with an empty tray and put in the rocks, pebbles and leaves. Put in a limited amount of water to form pool areas, add the green food colouring. Add the crocodiles.

What to do
Ask the children if there is a way to cross the swamp without getting caught by the crocodiles. Let them explore some ideas and if nobody suggests it tell them that they could use a raft and ask how they think they would make one.

Encourage them to try out the different materials (paper, plastic, wool, card and wood). What happens to the different materials? Which would be the best one?

Questions to ask
Where do crocodiles like to live? Where do they hide? How could you cross the swamp without getting caught by the crocodiles? If you made the water deeper what would happen to the crocodile?

For younger children
Introduce and use the words float, sink, deep, light and heavy. Ask the children to push down hard on one of the objects that floats very well. Can they feel anything pushing back? What do they think it is?

For older children
Increase the vocabulary to include surface, shallow, submerge. Use everyday objects and sort them into two sets – those that will float and those that sink. Ask the children to try to sink those that float. How many crocodiles do you need to put on to a raft to make it sink? Are there any objects they cannot sink?

Follow-up activities
● Make a model of a crocodile from clay, Plasticine or play dough. Will it float or sink?
● Read the story *Have you Seen the Crocodile?* by Colin West (Walker Books).

Develop fine motor skills with precision activities such as 'Catch the spider' and think big with expressive large movement in 'Phantom painter'. The eight activities in this chapter provide a range of ideas designed to develop all the children's physical abilities.

WATER WHEEL

Learning objective
To use fine motor skills to investigate the flow of water.

Group size
Up to four children.

What you need
A collection of plastic water wheels, small jugs, picture of water wheels, large pebbles, food colouring (optional), water tray, large bucket or bowl, sand, salt.

Setting up
Start with an empty tray. Place a water wheel in the tray and arrange pebbles around the base to support it. Position another water wheel in another part of the water tray. Fill a large bucket or bowl with water and place it under or near the tray. Put the jugs in the water ready.

What to do
Show the children the water wheels and demonstrate how they work, pouring gently and encouraging the children to watch, then repeat the process, but pour more quickly.

Introduce the idea of 'speed' as a force which the children can control by physical actions. Look at the different kinds of wheels and ask them if they think the same things will happen and why they think that? Allow the children to explore and experiment. Show them how to hold the jug at different heights and positions.

Questions to ask
What will happen when the water meets the wheel? How can you make the wheel go faster/slower?

For younger children
Younger children will find this physically demanding but it provides a good opportunity to 'teach' children safe grips and how to tip heavy things carefully in order to stay in control. Repeating the pouring and refilling will be the main physical options at this stage.

For older children
Older children could try out other materials such as sand with the water wheels. Pouring and filling and physical control can be observed for assessment purposes during this activity. Watch how the children grip and control.

Follow-up activities
● Use information books to find out more about water mills, and make a visit to a water mill if possible.
● Use old pipes and gutterings outside to watch how water flows and how you can change its directions.

CATCH THE SPIDER

Learning objective
To experience and use tools in order to improve fine motor skills.

Group size
Small groups or individuals.

What you need
A large or small water tray filled with water, blue or red food colouring, some plastic spiders, spaghetti (optional) a collection of kitchen tools, such as: spaghetti tongs, masher and fish slice.

Setting up
Add the food colouring to the water in the tray. Include the spaghetti at this stage, if you are using it. Place the spiders in the bottom of the tray. Place the tools around the side of the tray.

What to do
Explain to the children that the spiders need to be captured from the river or swamp. Tell them that they can use the tools as they do not know what might be in the water.

Let each child choose a tool and each try to capture a spider. They may wish to try a variety of tools. Watch how the children hold the tools and manage the task. Once they have captured a spider they can throw it back in and start again to catch another using a different tool.

Questions to ask
Where is the spider hiding? How could you get him out without touching the water? How did the spider get into the river/swamp? Where do spiders really live?

For younger children
Keep the water fairly shallow with younger children. If they are alarmed about the use of spiders use some different plastic insects or animals and consider using small dipper nets or sieves so that the children do not get disheartened if they find the tools difficult to use.

For older children
Use deeper, darker water so the task is more difficult. Allow the children to be more independent and allow them to experiment with their own ideas. Use different tools with the older child and allow them to make their own devices, experimenting with string and wood.

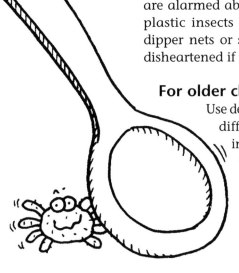

Follow-up activities
● Collect pictures and information about spiders and their homes.
● Make a collection of songs and nursery rhymes with spiders in.
● Pretend to be spiders and make a web with string.

APPLE BOBBING

Learning objective
To develop control of
body movements.

Group size
Individuals with the
other children
watching.

What you need
A large bowl of water, apples (one per child), table tennis balls, cotton reels, ice-cubes and food colouring, a towel.

Setting up
Make sure the bowl and the apples are clean. Fill the bowl with water. Put in about four or five of the apples. If splashes are a problem, protect the surrounding area with wads of newspaper. Prepare the ice-cubes by colouring and freezing them the night before.

What to do
Explain to the children they should try to catch one of the floating apples without using their hands. Remind them to keep their hands behind their back. The activity appears to be simple but it needs good balance and control to catch an apple. Have the towel ready to dry the children's faces when they have had a turn. (CARE! Some children may not like the idea of getting their faces wet.)

Remind the children that we should only taste or eat what we know is food and that nothing else should ever be put in mouths.

Replenish the apple stocks in the water as the children take their turns. Let them eat the apples when they have captured them!

Questions to ask
How will you get the apple? Why was it hard to catch the apple? What happened when you touched the apple?

For younger children
If younger children do not want to put their faces in the water, you could use a table tennis ball which they can blow across the surface of the water. Let them join with other children to eat the apples at the end of the activity.

For older children
Try floating coloured ice-cubes on the water and letting older children try to catch these in their mouths. Encourage them to tell you if this is easier or harder than catching the apples.

Follow-up activities
● Try a variety of things to float on the surface. Which ones are the easiest to catch?

MILKSHAKES

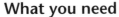

Learning objective
To use fine motor skills.

Group size
Small group.

What you need
A collection of small milk cartons, plastic bottles, drinking tumblers or plastic glasses, aprons and paper hats, white paint, icing sugar or cornflour. (CARE! Explain that they must not drink the water and watch to make sure younger children do not do so).

Setting up
The water tray is going to be the filling area in a milkshake factory and the children will need to wear a uniform to work in the factory (the apron and hat). Alongside the tray a table or shelf will be needed. On this will be all the empty containers. Paper and pencils and adhesive sticks could be added so that the children can make labels if they wish.

What to do
Explain that the water tray is now a place where milk or milkshake is being put into containers. The children need to pour 'milk' into the containers – they can use any of the containers, but the 'milk' must be filled to the top, as they all need to be exactly the same.
They will need to concentrate very carefully and hold the containers they pour with very carefully.

Questions to ask
How do you buy your milk at home, in bottles or cartons? How can you tell how much is left in a carton? What flavours can you put in milk? Can you pour it exactly?

For younger children
Younger children will probably be content to fill and empty cartons without specific measuring. Role-play with them and ask them for a pint of milk and let them serve you.

For older children
Older children can complete the job by designing and making labels for their milkshakes. They may also like to seal the containers with foil and Sellotape.

> **Follow-up activities**
> ● Look at containers that are linked with milk, the old glass bottle, an old milk churn, buckets that were carried by milking maids.
> ● Try some taste testing with real milkshake. What are the children's favourite flavours?
> ● Practise whisking milk using a fork or hand whisks. This would be an opportunity to observe skills with hand tools by children.
> ● Use the photocopiable sheet on page 64 to encourage attention to detail.

FILL IT UP

Learning objective
*To encourage
co-ordination and
concentration skills.*

Group size
Four to six children.

What you need
A water tray, a selection of containers such as: jugs, bowls, cups, egg cups, bottle funnels, tubes, bucket, washing-up liquid bottles with nozzles intact. Access to water supply. Mop and bucket to cope with spills. (CARE! Do not use any glass containers!)

Setting up
Put out an empty water tray or large bowl/baby's bath. Have some of the containers on show but keep some in reserve.

What to do
Ask the children how they can fill up the water tray/baby's bath. Support their suggestions wherever possible by providing the resources.
   Once the water tray has been filled allow them to play with the water and the containers, emptying and filling. Intervene with questions and introduce some different containers to extend the play.

Questions to ask
What is the best thing to use to fill the water tray? Why does the water spill when you carry it?

For younger children
Carrying containers full of liquid requires skill and concentration as well as strength and so you will have some spilling. Lend a guiding hand when necessary. Encourage younger children to use squeezy bottles which require a good firm grip and pressure to get the water out.

For older children
Increase their vocabulary to include the following words: brim, level, shallow, deep, light, heavy, enough. Use smaller containers which require more precision and see if they can find ways of filling narrow necked bottles. Demonstrate how you can fill a bottle by pushing it under the water. Let them feel the pressure pushing the bottle upwards.

Follow-up activities
● Make a milk bar –
filling and emptying
bottles.
● Experiment with
filling and emptying
containers using
tubing. Show how by
sucking you can draw
the water through.

PHANTOM PAINTER

Learning objective
To develop control and manipulation of tools. To develop large muscle movement.

Group size
Pairs.

What you need
Bucketfuls of water, apron, sponge, large brushes such as wallpapering brushes, household painting brushes, small brushes.

Setting up
This activity is best done outdoors. It can be linked with any decorating work happening within your site or at any of the children's homes. Keep the resources in the large bucket ready for a suitable opportunity to work outside.

What to do
Supply the materials and tell the children you need to 'paint' the walls and doors outside. Let them work in pairs co-operating with each other and using all the tools available. Encourage them to put some enthusiasm in and to use their whole bodies in wide sweeping movements to cover all the surface area as quickly as possible.

Show them how to use the smaller brushes to deal with smaller areas such as doors and frames and how to be more careful and precise in working on these areas.

Questions to ask
What has happened to the water. Where has it gone? Does it make the same marks on all the walls?

For younger children
Younger children can be restricted to 'painting' the large areas of the walls reaching and stretching their whole body with large open movements. Let them use the sponges for washing and cleaning outside.

For older children
Let older children work on different surface textures. Encourage them to work at different levels using blocks or a nursery ladder with adult supervision, to climb. Provide some objects that will require more precise skills and smaller brushes, such as the nursery furniture or play house furniture. Allow them to choose the most suitable brush for the job.

Follow-up activities
● Provide a worker's tidy box, filled with household odds and ends so that they can play at being DIY experts!
● Fix up large sheets of paper to a fence or wall outside and let the children paint large scale pictures. This is good practise for wide arm movements.
● Use damp paper, large brushes and ink or paint. The wetter the paper the greater the spread of the paint.

PADDLING POOL

Learning objective
To use the whole body in water and to explore water play with large muscle skills.

Group size
Depending on the pool size but with several adult helpers at all times for safety. (CARE! Drowning can occur in very shallow water.)

What you need
A safe place outside to set up. Paddling pool, pump, water, some selected water toys. Either water mammals for an imaginative environment or more skill-based objects such as sieves and water wheels. Bathing suits and towels.

Setting up
Filling up the pool takes time so either decide to fill it up before the children arrive or incorporate the filling process into the activity. If you decide to involve the children they could help with their own buckets or you could use a hose or adult buckets. Place the equipment on the outside of the pool to prevent children jumping in and hurting themselves on the equipment.

What to do
Change into bathing suits. Restrict the play to a limited number of children at a time, to suit the size of the pool and the number of helpers available. Before they go into the water establish which children have had a lot or a little experience of water and those who are apprehensive.

Ask the children to move their arms up and down and pretend to swim with their arms to warm them up. Then ask them to lift their legs up and down. Encourage them to shake their arms, bodies, heads and feet. Introduce a song such as 'heads, shoulders, knees and toes'.

Allow them time for free play in the pool and then introduce the water toys.

Make sure there is plenty of time to dry and dress and encourage the children to do it for themselves.

Questions to ask
What must we not do when we play in the water? Is the water deep or shallow? If someone is frightened what should you do? How many buckets did it take to fill the pool?

For younger children
Experience in water will be more relevant than age in this activity. Let younger children play with watering cans and items that pour and fill.

For older children
Older children will enjoy using a paddling pool as an imaginative environment and could use water mammals to create a pretend play setting. They could also use props like small dipper nets to catch the toys with or to be fishermen.

Follow-up activities
● Tell traditional 'water' stories for example *Jonah and the Whale*.
● Make a pretend swimming baths with an office to buy a ticket, a locker to put your clothes in (a cardboard box) and a life-guard.
● Make a seaside outside. Put pebbles and pretend seaweed in the water.

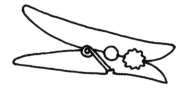

WASHDAY BLUES

Learning objective
To develop fine motor skills and to select appropriate tools.

Group size
Up to four children.

What you need

Water tray, pegs and a washing line, empty soap powder packets (well rinsed), soap, mild liquid detergent, some clothes which need to be washed, clothes basket, scrubbing brushes, hand cream/lotion, towel.

Setting up

Provide sufficient space around the water tray for the children to move freely about. Fill the water tray with warm water. Fix up the washing line.

What to do

Start off by showing the children the dirty clothes, explain that you need to wash them and ask the children what you should do.

Ask the children to help you sort the clothes ready for washing. Sort them in to piles of all white and coloured. Discuss why you need to sort them. As you wash the clothes use the appropriate vocabulary: squeeze, soap suds, rinse, hang out.

Demonstrate how the clothes

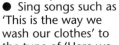

must go through a particular sequence – water, detergent, scrub, rinse and peg out. Help to sustain the play by introducing different cleaning agents such as the liquid detergent and the soap (CARE! Some children have allergies to soap products). Let the children pretend to use the washing powder. When the children have finished tip away the soapy water and provide clear water for rinsing everything. Help the children to peg the garments out to dry.

Encourage the children to work co-operatively with each other and with you. Make sure all the children dry their hands well.

Questions to ask

How do the clothes get dirty? How do the clothes feel when they are in the water? (Heavy, slimy, smooth, slippery.) How do your hands feel in the water? What do the clothes look like when they are dry?

For younger children

Younger children will love to put their hands into the soapy water. Grasping the scrubbing brushes with their small fingers may be difficult for them. Use words like scrubbing and rinsing as you play.

For older children

Ask older children to select appropriate methods and equipment for cleaning the different garments. They will be using fine muscles to grasp the brush and to scrub. Lifting and carrying the basket and stretching to peg out all give good exercise to the upper body.

Follow up
● Sing songs such as 'This is the way we wash our clothes' to the tune of 'Here we go round the mulberry bush'. Let the children suggest extra verses and do the actions together.
● Mime specific washing actions for the children and ask them to say what you are doing.
● Say the poems 'Washing day' and 'Blanket' from *Teaching Speech and Drama in the Infant School* by Penny Whittam (Ward Lock).

CREATIVE DEVELOPMENT

A colourful approach to water is examined in this chapter. Using a range of materials and tools the children will have the opportunity to develop their creative skills. Activities include a one-colour experience in 'It's a colourful world' and creating a winter wonderland in 'Iceland'.

MARBLE GOO

Learning objective
To explore colour and pattern.

Group size
Individuals, pairs or small group of four to six children.

What you need
You can buy specially prepared inks for marbling or try to make your own, (see recipe below). A water tray, wallpaper paste, waterproof inks, droppers, paper, newspaper.

Setting up
Half fill the water tray. Have the inks and droppers ready for use and the newspaper near by to put the wet pictures on. Cut to size different types of paper (absorbent, thin, thick and glossy).

What to do
Demonstrate to the children how to drop small amounts of ink onto the surface of the water, then let the children try themselves. The ink will float and as the oil moves quickly across the water it creates unpredictable beautiful patterns. Introduce a second colour. (Use black ink sparingly as it can take over!)

Encourage the children to talk about the swirling patterns. Hold some paper in the centre and gently lay it on top of the water, it will quickly absorb the pattern. Remove it and place on top of newspaper to dry. The oil moves to the sides of the tray and collects there. As the children work you will need to renew the colours. It is interesting to see how the colours change from strong to pale on repeat printings.

Questions to ask
What has happened to the paint? Why do you think it is happening? Have you seen patterns like this before?

For younger children
Help younger children to place their paper on top of the water. It will require skill to hold it in place and to remove it carefully. Use the patterns for background displays or to cover the children's books.

For older children
Help the children create patterns on their paper which suggest movements (water, clouds, swirls and sea pictures). Use these as a stimulus and let the children add to the pictures when they are dry, using colour inks and paints or use them as a base for a collage. Cut and stick the patterns to make new pictures.

Follow-up activities
● Marbling ink recipe – mix two tablespoons of powder paint with two tablespoons of vegetable oil. (CARE! You can add one tablespoon of turps).
● Drop paints onto thick wallpaper paste and use a comb to swirl some colours.
● Mix cornflour paste with water and food colouring in a large container. Make sure it is thick and smooth. This mixture runs through the fingers almost like a liquid but appears to be solid when in the tray.

THE BOTTLE SHOP

Learning objective
To use the senses to explore colour change.

Group size
Small group, pairs or individuals.

What you need
Water tray or individual plastic trays for individuals. A collection of small bottles and containers, food colouring, paint, wax crayons, paper, droppers or bottles with small holes in the top. Food flavourings – peppermint, banana.

Setting up
Use a water tray with a small amount of water or individual plastic trays, so that each child can explore the materials and produce a more individual piece of work. Prepare the food colouring and weak paint solution in the bottles/droppers. Cut paper to size if needed. Put two or three drops of food flavouring into some of the bottles.

What to do
Examine the bottles and containers with the children and then ask them to very carefully trickle drops of coloured water onto the surface of the water and to gently stir it with one finger. Observe what happens. Add another colour and mix the two colours gently together. Watch the swirls and twists that occur. Once the children have seen and talked about this ask them to capture the effect on paper using wax crayons or paints.

Experiment further by dropping paint onto different types of paper – filter/blotting paper, good/poor quality paper. Let the children use their fingers to make interesting swirls and patterns.

Questions to ask
Ask the children to describe the colours and the smells in the bottles. Do the smells remind them of anything? What do they think will happen when the two colours meet?

For younger children
The task of tipping and dropping the paint onto the surface of the water may be difficult for younger children so provide adult help if necessary. Remind the children of some key words to describe their work, such as pattern and swirl.

For older children
Increase the vocabulary relating to colour mixing. Explore wax resist painting using the wax crayons and a tray of blue paints to resemble the sea.

Follow-up activities
● Try squeezing and swirling paint from bottles. Restrict the colours and make volcano pictures using only yellow and orange. Create firework pictures using the wax resist technique or just make abstract patterns.
● Mix blues and make swirls like a whirlpool/puddle.

ITALIA

Learning objective
To explore a variety of materials and textures.

Group size
Small group.

What you need
A water tray, a selection of dried pasta, food colouring, kitchen utensils (drainers, spaghetti tongs), aprons.

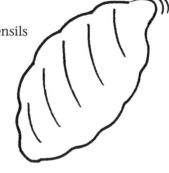

Setting up
Fill the water tray up and add some food colouring. Put out the dried pasta on a table or nearby surface and arrange the tools around the tray.

What to do
Let the children use all their senses (except taste!) to explore some dried pasta. Tell them to notice its texture, shape and colour. Ask them to put pasta in the water tray themselves or watch you do it if they are apprehensive about this (some children do not like doing this part of the activity but will join in when the opportunity to use the utensils is offered).

They will have noticed the colour of the water already and may ask you if the pasta will change colour or not. (You would need to add a large amount of colouring for this to occur).

Ask the children to describe what happens to the pasta in the water, and to tell you how it feels now compared with how it felt before, when it was dry.

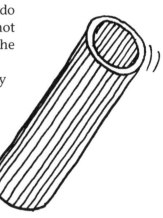

Questions to ask
What colour is the water today? Do you know how I made this happen? What is this called? (Investigating the pasta). Have you seen it before? Do you like it when it's cooked?

For younger children
Allow the children to play with the pasta and encourage vocabulary such as 'cold, slimy, like snakes', to evolve. Let them try to capture/grab/collect the pasta pieces.

For older children
Use different shaped and coloured pasta and encourage sorting. Introduce sieves and other tools so the children have to select the best tool for collection.

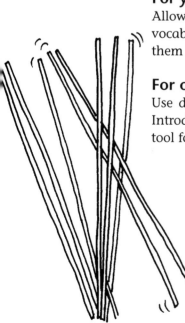

Follow-up activities
● Let the children experiment adding food colouring to bowls of water.
● Thread pasta to make bracelets and necklaces.
● Read *Magic Pasta Pot* by Tomi de Paola (Andersen Press) or *Spaghetti for Susy* by Peta Coplans (Mammoth).

JELLY WOBBLE

Learning objective
To observe colour
change through first
hand experiences.

Group size
Small or medium
group or individual if
adequate resources are
available.

What you need
A selection of jelly packets of at least three different colours and water
which is warm/hot, a clear bowl/tank/water tray, some wooden
spoons or utensils. (CARE! Constant supervision is required at all
times and especially in the early stages of the activity.)

Setting up
Timing is crucial, set up as close to the children's arrival
as possible. Warm water needs to be poured into the
water tray.

What to do
Ask the children to choose or collect jelly cubes of varying colours.
They can then place their cubes in the water carefully, using the
wooden spoon. Remind them to remember which is their cube and to
watch it carefully to see what happens as their cube dissolves.
As the water cools the children may wish to try and mix the
water around. Encourage the children to talk about what is
happening.
Following this ask the children to repeat their observations
and represent them with paint. Use a small amount of dry
paint on paper and then add water. Ask them to move the
paper around with their hands slowly tipping it from side to
side and watching the colours merge.

Questions to ask
What is happening? Where is the colour coming from? Where is it
going? Can you mix paint like this? What happens if we mix it up?
How does jelly get its colour?

For younger children
The children will gain from the process
of watching and mixing their cubes and
noticing the changes as the cubes melt.
Make sure the children aren't tempted to
put the jelly in their mouths! Encourage
them to put the cubes in a different part
of the tray to see what will happen.

For older children
Ask older children to try to make a
rainbow collection or to mix favourite
colours up. Do the same exercise with
frozen ice-cubes in different colours and
ask them to observe the colours. Will the
result and process be the same?

Follow-up activities
● Investigate colour
and effect. Use other
food for example,
coloured pasta.
Leave to dry and use
for collage.
● Melt some jelly
cubes ready for the
children to place
them on paper. Let
them mix up the
colours and
experiment. Leave
them to dry.

WHISK

Learning objective
*To explore the concept
of mixing and texture.*

Group size
*Small group with a
water tray, or
individuals with plastic
trays.*

What you need
A selection of household hand whisks, paintbrushes, low plastic trays, paint, tools that are linked to mixing such as forks and spoons. A water tray or water in a low tray to stimulate mixing. Food colouring.

Setting up
Put water in the water tray and arrange the various whisks/tools in and on the side of the water.

What to do
Tell the children that you are going to do some mixing using different things. Allow the children to begin using the hand whisks in the water tray. They will enjoy the noise of the water and the whisk, and this provides a useful opportunity to develop hand and eye control. Now add food colouring and allow the children to observe what is happening. If you intend to repeat this with follow-on groups, start the activity with the lightest colour.

Encourage the children to say 'mix' and develop a rhyme or saying to say as they work. Then allow them to use a fork and a whisk in a low tray with some different coloured paint in and to mix it up. Once they have finished whisking on top of the tray take a contact print of the whisk pictures.

The dirty whisk can be reused by the next group in the water tray and the activity can continue. The experience will allow children to explore colour mixing, tools and surface medium.

Questions to ask
What is the tool called? What is it used for? How does it work? What marks does it make? What has happened to the paint? What kind of picture has it made?

For younger children
Start younger children off with simpler tools such as a fork or spoon or a simple hand whisk. These tools will all make a mark and this will enable children to see cause and effect with the paint and also develop hand and eye co-ordination skills.

For older children
Some older children will know their colours and will be used to mixing different ones with a paintbrush so using a whisk will give them an opportunity to extend their skills. They could add glitter or adhesive to their mixes too.

Follow-up activities
● Mix together adhesive and sawdust.
● Put in wallpaper paste and red food colouring! Mix it up and make patterns.
● Try some recipes that involve whisking, such as meringues and batter.

IT'S A COLOURFUL WORLD

Learning objective
To explore colour using sensory experiences.

Group size
Individuals or small groups.

What you need
Provide a total colour environment by using objects all in the same colour range (jugs, funnels, and sieves), a water tray, food colouring, jelly, water toys, transparent containers, plain and coloured paper, absorbent paper such as coffee filter paper or paper hand towels, droppers, a piece of white cotton cloth for each child, a pot of water.

Setting up
Fill the water tray and mix in food colouring. Put in the play objects and the transparent containers.

What to do
Let the children explore their colourful environment! They can enjoy playing in the water, filling, pouring and funnelling. Listen to their comments about the colour. After they have had some free play be prepared to intervene with questions about the colours and to develop their play ideas. Let them dip their piece of white cloth into the water and see how it absorbs the colour.

Questions to ask
What is different about the water today? Do you know the name for this colour? What else do you know which is this colour? Do you have a favourite colour? Can you show me something in the same colour? Can you match the colour to something in the room?

For younger children
Let them explore the coloured water, watching it trickle and move in the tray. Work with younger children and show them how to use the dropper to drip some of the coloured water onto damp paper. Watch what happens and ask them to tell you what they can see.

For older children
Fold a filter paper into eight squares and dip each corner into a different colour and open it out. Some of the colours will have blended. Help them to find names for their colours by association, such as daffodil yellow and marmalade orange.

Follow-up activities
● Paint a picture using only one colour and display with a caption – 'Michael's cherry coloured picture'.
● Let the children paint one hand in one colour and make a hand print, paint the other hand a different colour and print with it. Next rub their two hands together and print. What has happened?

ICELAND

Learning objective
*To provide the
opportunity to think
about other
environments. To
create another world.*

Group size
*Small groups of four to
six children.*

What you need
A large cement mixing tray, salt or bath crystals, water, a selection of
play penguins and fish, vegetable colouring, coloured inks, books
and pictures of cold countries.

Setting up
Put some of the play animals into containers with water and freeze
them overnight. Freeze a quantity of ice-cubes, using a variety of
different shaped containers. Put some water into the tray but do not
cover it too deeply. Leave one end dry and cover this with salt. Build
up the ice-cubes to represent icebergs. Take the frozen animals out of
their containers. If you have snow outside bring a bucketful in and
let the children include this in their play.

What to do
Tell the children that you are going to create a winter scene together.
Make sure they only handle the icy shapes for a short time to prevent
them hurting their fingers and keep a supply of towels close by to dry
hands immediately. Introduce the colourings as an additional factor
and let the colour mix with the salt. Point out to the children how the
colour is absorbed by the salt.

Listen to what the children say as they work and encourage them to
improvise an imaginary story with the characters and shapes available.

Questions to ask
What do your hands feel like? How do you think the animals keep
warm? What has made the ice? Where does it go to? What makes it
melt? Look at the salt and talk about it dissolving. Where is it going
to? What will happen to the snow in the bucket?

For younger children
Model things for younger children to imitate.
Let them take over the role of the fish,
swimming them in and out of the water.

For older children
Let them arrange and rearrange the
materials. What happens when
you put salt or colouring on
the ice? Increase their
vocabulary by asking
them to describe the
ice-cubes as they
melt.

Follow-up activities
● Make a shiny
collection or an ice
grotto in the play
area.
● Make icicles out of
blue Cellophane and
metallic paper to
hang from the
windows.

I'M A LITTLE TEAPOT

Learning objective
To encourage
imaginative play using
a familiar experience.

Group size
A group of between
four and six children
around the water tray.

What you need
A water tray, a collection of containers for filling and pouring, a selection of tea-leaves and tea-bags, spoons, play tea-cups, sieves, strainers, filter paper and funnel, aprons.

Setting up
Fill the water tray. Have the different teas in see-through containers close to the play area. Ensure the children wear aprons.

What to do
This is essentially a free activity for the children to explore. Encourage them to pretend to make and serve cups of tea. They will have the opportunity of stirring and measuring. They will see the dry leaves change in texture and colour once they become wet. The leaves can be sieved, dried and used again.

Questions to ask
Ask the children to describe what they are going to do. What do they notice? Why does this happen? What sort of tea do they use at home? Some of the children may use tea-bags, others may boil the tea in a saucepan depending on their cultural backgrounds.

For younger children
Whilst playing the younger children will be gaining skills of tipping and pouring. Encourage one-to-one matching, cup to person or cups to number in the group.

For older children
Look at samples of different tea. Notice the similarities and differences, size and colour, the smells. How can you separate the tea-leaves from the water? Try different methods, a strainer, filter paper and funnel, a sieve. Why would you want to separate them? Talk about the steps to follow when making a cup of tea. Why is it important to get the order right?

Follow-up activities
● Use the tea-leaves to make pictures. Drop tea stains onto fabric and make patterns. Send to the class laundry to be made clean. (See page 17.)
● Find out where tea comes from. (A bush.) Find out which countries are famous for growing tea.
● Read the story *The Tiger who came to tea*, Judith Kerr (Picture Lions).
● Learn the poem 'I'm a little teapot'.

PHOTOCOPIABLES

Name _____

Finish the pictures.

Name _____

Draw a cup to go with each bottle.

Draw an arrow to match up the bottles.

Name _____

How many?

4

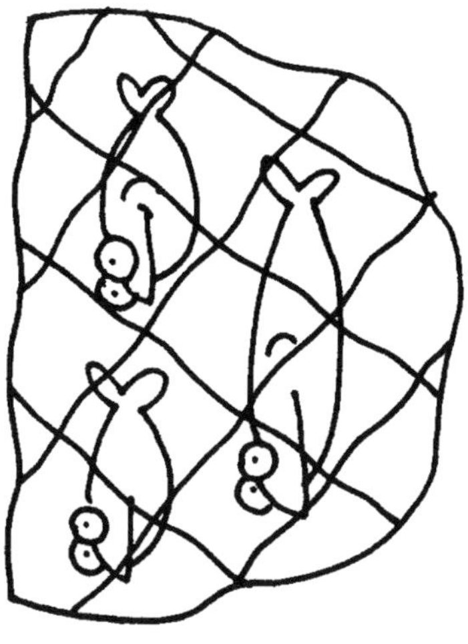

How many?

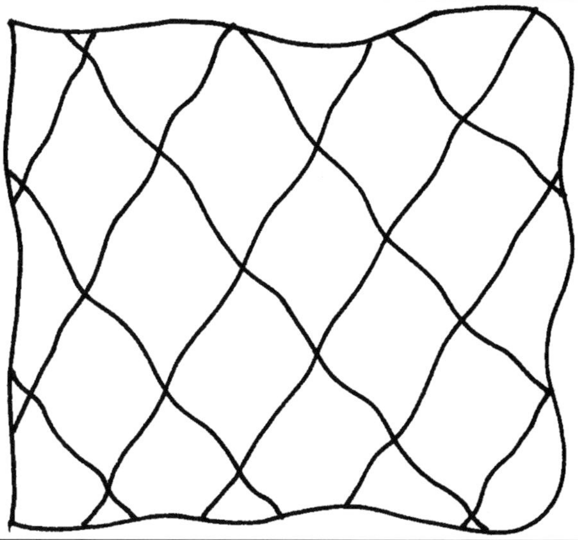

6

How many fish have been caught?

How many?

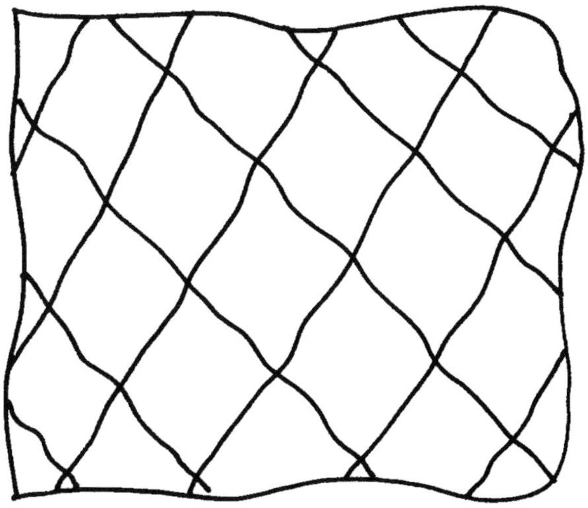

Draw in the fish.

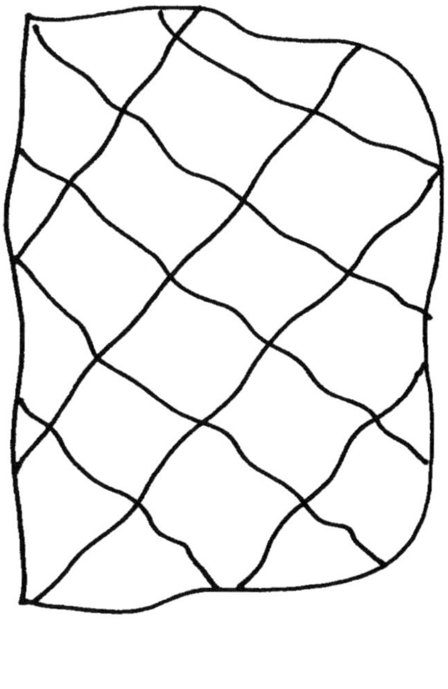

2

Name _____

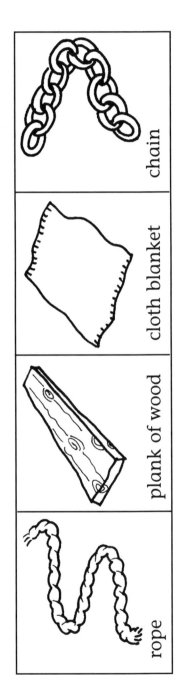

What could you use to help?

chain

cloth blanket

plank of wood

rope

Choose one of these things and draw it on the picture to save the pirate's friend.

Cut out the pictures and put them in the right order.

Name _____

Spot the odd one out in each row and colour it a different colour to the rest.